Telephone and Reception Skills

David Alexander

MULTILEVEL BUSINESS ENGLISH PROGRAMME

PHOENIX
ELT

incorporating
PRENTICE HALL MACMILLAN

New York   London   Toronto   Sydney   Tokyo   Singapore

Published 1995 by Phoenix ELT
Campus 400, Spring Way
Maylands Avenue, Hemel Hempstead
Hertfordshire, HP2 7EZ

A division of Prentice Hall International (UK) Ltd

Illustrations by Art Construction and Bill Piggins

Printed and bound in Great Britain

British Library Cataloguing in Publication Data
A catalogue record for this book is available from the British Library

ISBN 0-13-461-6332

5   4   3   2   1
99 98 97 96 95

Produced by **AMR**

Acknowledgements
The author and publishers acknowledge, with grateful thanks, the following bibliographical references and sources.
NVQ level 2 Administration (2nd ed), L. Bourne and P. Scott, Pitman 1994
Practical Office Skills, C. Taylor, McGraw-Hill 1991
Secretarial Procedures for the Electronic Office (2nd ed), R. Kutie and J. Rhodes, Wiley 1986
Secretarial Procedures, T. Foster, Stanley Thornes 1990
Senior Secretarial Duties and Office Organisation (3rd ed), E. Austin, Pitman 1974

Kirby College, Middlesbrough
Oxford College of Further Education
Joanna Cairns

The author and publishers wish to acknowledge with thanks the following photographic sources:
Stuart Boreham Photography p7, 10, 14, 17, 19, 22, 25, 28, 31, 33 × 4, 37, 41, 44; Greg Evans International p42 × 3, 43 ×3

The author and publishers are grateful to Rosemary McClintock, Area Co-ordinator (Administration) at Oxford College of Further Education for her helpful comments.

CONTENTS

INTRODUCTION

INTRODUCTION

WHO IS THE BOOK FOR?

The book and the accompanying tape are primarily for non-native speakers of English, who are already in, or about to enter, reception work in an institution or office, and who need competence in English language skills in order to do their work more effectively. Reference to the specific language of restaurant and hotel reception is not included.

The material constitutes one of a series of modules accompanying the **Multi-level Business English Programme**. It can be used as a supplement to the **MBEP** course by students needing more practice in the specific or semi-technical areas of telephone and reception work, or quite independently of the core course.

WHAT ARE THE AIMS?

The aims are:

- to present a wide range of language associated with reception work, both the language *of* and *about* reception.

- to develop an understanding and use of key vocabulary.

- to develop an understanding of incoming telephone calls and of the face-to-face language of internal and external callers and visitors, who use English as a native or international language.

- to develop an understanding of English language documents that are common to reception work.

- to develop appropriate and correct responses to telephone callers and visitors.

HOW IS THE BOOK ORGANISED?

The book is modular to enable users to focus on the practice they need most and to enter and exit where they wish. It is *not* necessary to start at Unit 1 and to work through to Unit 12.

The language in the book is *target language* and *contextual language,* i.e. the focus is sometimes on the principal phraseology that is heard and spoken in reception work, and sometimes on the language concerned with the subject of reception.

There are four parts to the book. Each part covers, more or less, the same job areas, but focuses on a different language development need related to these areas.

Part One presents a general overview of the area of reception work. It includes short, written or recorded extracts from authentic material, prepared for native English-speaking receptionists and students of reception. The purpose is not to teach students in English what they may already know in their own language, but to familiarise them with the terminology and phraseology of the profession. It consists of textual exposition and information about reception work for reading, discussion, comprehension and vocabulary extension.

Part Two exposes users to recordings of face-to-face and telephone exchanges between receptionists and callers or visitors, in order for them to familiarise themselves with the spoken language and to check their understanding, inferential or interpretive skills, and their ability to take appropriate action.

Part Three develops accuracy and communicative competence in the spoken language of responding to, and initiating information from, callers and visitors.

Part Four is a reference section offering access to the useful phrases covered in the book, the tapescript and an answer key to the exercises.

WHAT ABOUT METHODOLOGY AND LEVEL?

The exercises can be done in class or in private study and are all aimed at the individual user, whether he/she is studying in class or not. In other words, the material can be used effectively with or without a teacher, but there are no group-work activities, although some exercises can be practised in pairs.

The exercises are both of the traditional and task-based type, i.e. care has been taken for the exercises, where possible, to reflect what receptionists have to do in their work, but there are some of the more mechanical language exercises as well. For example, in Part Three, there are some traditional transformation exercises. These are not included just for the sake of transformation, but because this type of exercise enables users to manipulate and vary their phraseology, which is what they have to do in the work.

The level is, broadly speaking, intermediate, but because students often have different levels themselves of receptive and productive language skills, there is a range of task level in the book. Consequently, some students will find some sections easier than others.

PART ONE

ABOUT RECEPTION

RECEPTION RESPONSIBILITIES

GENERAL RESPONSIBILITIES

Pre-reading

Make your own short list of a receptionist's general responsibilities.

Which of these words would you expect to find in the following texts about responsibilities?

> visitors   invoices   typing   welcome
> security   filing

Reading

Read the descriptions of the main general duties of a receptionist. How do they compare with your own list? Do you disagree with any of them?

The receptionist must act as an interface between the organisation and the outside world, receive visitors, with and without appointments, and direct them accordingly, act as a filter and security screen, entertain guests where necessary, keep a record of callers and receive parcels. In addition, receptionists often operate as relief telephonists and may undertake general typing and clerical duties, depending on the nature of the organisation.

Most organisations like to enjoy good public relations. The way in which visitors are received can influence their impression of the company, so receptionists should be efficient and make visitors feel welcome.

1 Find words in the texts which can be replaced by the following words without a change in meaning: *affect, secretarial, opinion, do.*

2 Find words or expressions in the texts which mean the same as:

  a look after visitors
  b an intermediary between the company and the public
  c help when the switchboard is busy
  d have a good image
  e a meeting with a fixed time and place

3 According to the text, why is the way in which a receptionist receives visitors important?

4 According to the text, how can the main duties of a receptionist differ, depending on the organisation?

SPECIFIC RESPONSIBILITIES

Pre-reading

Make your own short list of specific responsibilities in reception work.

Reading

Match the duties with the circumstances.

Which of the duties do you think receptionists should **not** be expected to handle?

DUTIES

1 Taking visitors' hats and coats
2 Keeping a record of all phone calls
3 Keeping a record of all visitors
4 Escorting visitors
5 Ordering taxis
6 Making tea and coffee
7 Handling payments
8 Giving travel information
9 Giving first-aid
10 Cleaning and tidying
11 Making social conversation with visitors and callers
12 Handling threatening calls
13 Looking after lost property
14 Routing calls
15 Signing for deliveries

CIRCUMSTANCES

a It is usual for visitors to be taken to the place of their appointment by the person they are meeting, or someone from that department.
b Vistors often ask the receptionist to arrange for this kind of transport.
c In smaller companies, receptionists can be expected to deal with refreshments for visitors.
d Receptionists are usually responsible for keeping their work station tidy.
e Receptionists should talk pleasantly to visitors, when time permits.
f In small or exclusive companies, receptionists may help visitors with their outer garments.
g It is unlikely that receptionists would have time for this.
h A Visitor's Register is common for this.
i Receptionists are not usually expected to deal with money.
j Most receptionists would be expected to cope with minor ailments or medical emergencies.
k It is quite common for receptionists to have to help callers and visitors with reaching and leaving the premises.
l In many companies, reception and switchboard duties are combined.
m The reception desk is a usual place for items that visitors leave behind.
n Receptionists working on the switchboard may have to deal with these, e.g. bomb threats.
o The reception desk is often the place where parcels and special couriers arrive.

1 Find words in the lists of duties and circumstances, which mean the same as:

> office desk area   building
> accompanying   clothing   illnesses

2 In what circumstances would receptionists be involved in the following duties? Use your own words as far as possible.

a helping visitors with public transport
b offering refreshments
c helping visitors with their coats, etc.
d making and receiving telephone calls

RECEPTIONISTS AS A SOURCE OF INFORMATION

In addition to having a wide range of duties, receptionists are often expected to be a source of information concerning many matters inside and outside the building.

1 Look at these examples of things that receptionists may be asked and prioritise them, from 1 to 14, from your own point of view.

- Current local weather forecast
- International time zones
- Telephone, fax and address details of hotels and restaurants
- Company sales figures
- National and international news
- Results of national and international sports events
- Local shopping information
- Names and positions of particular members of staff
- Addresses, phone and fax numbers of other local or international offices
- Details of local dental or medical facilities
- Location of particular departments in the building
- Location of toilets
- Directions for getting to local, national or international locations
- Location of refreshment facilities, locally or in the building

2 Can you list other types of information that receptionists may be asked to provide?

RECEIVING VISITORS

Pre-reading

Make your own short list of the types of visitors that receptionists meet in their work.

Which of these words would you expect to find in the following text about visitors at reception? Why?

> *representatives   interviewees*
> *maintenance   police*

Reading

Here are some examples of types of visitors at reception and their reasons for visiting. How do they compare with your own list?

Visitors with appointments

Job applicants attending interviews (interviewees)

Representatives from other firms, attending meetings or offering services

Other people attending meetings

Visitors without appointments

Sales representatives selling goods and services

People enquiring about job vacancies

People making general enquiries

Regular and official callers

People handling the delivery of goods and mail (e.g. postal workers, couriers)

Service personnel (e.g. maintenance engineers, cleaning and catering contractors)

Personal callers (e.g. friends and family of staff)

Official visitors (e.g. police, fire, ambulance services, inspectors, government officials)

1 Describe, in your own words, each of the three types of visitor referred to above.

2 Check you know the meaning of these words in the text above. Then use them to complete the gaps in the sentences.

> *delivery   regular   vacancies*
> *firms   goods*

a People interested in work should ask about ... in the company.
b Do ... visitors have to sign in at reception?
c Receptionists often sign for the receipt of certain ... .
d The Reception desk is often the place for the ... of letters and parcels.
e Large international ... are often difficult to get into.

3 In your opinion, what types of visitor would receptionists usually allow to bypass normal reception procedures?

RECEPTION SKILLS AND QUALITIES

WHAT MAKES A GOOD RECEPTIONIST?

Pre-reading

Make your own short list of what you consider to be the qualities of a good receptionist.

Study the list below and put a tick (✓) against those you think are necessary qualities or requirements and a cross (✗) against those you think are unimportant or unnecessary. Add others to your list.

> attractive   smartly dressed   efficient   discreet
> ambitious   non-smoker   eloquent   cheerful
> good posture

Reading

Read these articles about the qualities of a good receptionist. What is your opinion about each of them?

Article 1

Appearance and initial impressions are everything, so a good receptionist should be pretty and smart. She should be well made-up and have well-manicured nails, well-brushed teeth and clean hands. She must be tidy, friendly and well-spoken. It is important that she is respectful to her superiors.

Article 2

A good receptionist should have the following: a neat appearance, a pleasant manner, a clear voice, a helpful attitude, tact, a calm and polite nature, a positive image, organisational skills, first-aid knowledge, knowledge of the company and its products, knowledge of staff and their responsibilities. He/she should always be anxious to help and be able to handle stressful situations, such as receiving several visitors simultaneously and remaining calm when telephone callers have to be kept on hold, for example.

Article 3

The person should have a good general education, with emphasis on good oral communication skills and human relations ability, a pleasant personality and attractive appearance and the ability to engage in easy but discreet conversation. In addition, he/she should be well-organised and efficient, have a good memory for names and faces and take an interest in people and in the organisation.

1   Find these words in the articles and guess their meaning if you are not sure. Then choose the best of the two meanings given.

   a   initial impressions (first feelings or opinions/early)

   b   well made-up (well-dressed/skilful use of cosmetics)

   c   well-spoken (speaking in a refined manner/admired)

   d   manner (behaviour/politeness)

e tact (curiosity/diplomacy)

f anxious (worried/keen)

g discreet (secretive/tactful)

2 Think about or discuss the answers to these questions arising from the articles.

  a How important is it for receptionists to be attractive and what does *attractive* mean ?

  b In your experience, are receptionists usually women? Why?

  c What makes a bad receptionist?

3 Note down some meanings, or examples, for these expressions in the articles:

  positive image, first-aid knowledge, good general education, human relations ability, ability to engage in easy but discreet conversation.

4 If you are already in reception work, or will soon be, list what you think are your own good and bad qualities in respect of the job. Compare your answers with a partner, if possible.

RECEPTION SKILLS

Study the list of reception skills and the associated functional situations and check you understand them all.

1 Match the skills with the functional situations.

2 Arrange the skills in order of priority for reception work and give your reasons.

Skills

a Eloquence/foreign language competence

b Good level of numeracy

c First-aid training

d Personnel/human resources training

e Good level of literacy

f Shorthand

g Business school training

h Computer skills

Functional situations

1 Note-taking

2 Speaking to international callers and visitors

3 Understanding invoices and accounts

4 Dealing with employees' requirements

5 Coping with minor ailments or emergencies

6 Identifying visitors' and callers' requirements in relation to company departments

7 Reading and writing with accuracy

8 Dealing with enquiries about information systems

A reception questionnaire

Tick (✓) what you do/would do in these circumstances.

1 You have a caller on the line who is complaining strongly about the time it took you to answer a call. Would you:
  a apologise and explain?
  b tell the caller that you are working as fast as you can and that everyone has to take his/her turn?
  c ask the caller to be more polite and patient?
  d other?

2 You have a visitor who hasn't made an appointment and who insists on seeing the Personnel Manager. Would you:
  a explain that meetings are not easy without an appointment and try to make an appointment for the person?
  b direct the person to the Personnel Department?
  c ask the visitor to leave?
  d other?

3 The telephone rings while you are dealing with a visitor. Would you:
  a ignore the phone until you have finished with the visitor?
  b Make excuses to your visitor and answer the phone?
  c take the phone off the hook?
  d other?

4 A visitor with an appointment has been waiting for more than 15 minutes. Would you:
  a do nothing?
  b call the person with whom the appointment was made?
  c escort the visitor to the person's office?
  d other?

5 The switchboard is very busy and visitors arriving at reception are beginning to queue. Would you:
  a attend to the visitors when the phone stops ringing?
  b leave the phone ringing and attend to the visitors?
  c ask the callers to hold the line while you attend to the visitors?
  d other?

6 You have a problem call from someone who says a bomb has been left in the building. Would you:
  a tell the person to go away and put the phone down?
  b sound the alarm?
  c follow company procedure, irrespective of your own views?
  d other?

7 A visitor with an appointment refuses to give you his/her name or to sign the Visitor's Register. Would you:
  a refuse to call the person with whom the appointment has been made, until the visitor co-operates?
  b do as the visitor wishes?
  c try and persuade the visitor to co-operate?
  d other?

8 A visitor asks if he/she can make a phone call from the reception desk. Would you:
  a agree?
  b refuse?
  c show the visitor where there is a payphone?
  d other?

9 A visitor or caller wants to speak to someone in the company about something, but he/she is very vague and doesn't know who to speak to. Would you:
  a put him/her onto anybody that seems free?
  b try to discover what the request concerns?
  c ask the person to call/come back when he/she can give you a name or department?
  d other?

10 A senior employee arrives and complains to you that someone has parked in his/her reserved parking space. Would you:
  a ask for the employee's car keys and say you will handle it?
  b sympathise but do nothing?
  c take the number of the offending vehicle and trace the driver?
  d other?

THE VISITOR'S REGISTER AND THE APPOINTMENTS BOOK

1 Study the extract from a Visitor's Register and the notes below, made by the receptionist. Summarise the entries and the notes as if you were briefing a colleague on the details. Work with a partner if possible.

e.g.: *At 9.15, Mr Zahos signed in, from Papadopoulos Ltd. His appointment was for 9.30 with Jackie Jones in Marketing. He was collected by Sarah de Souza. He signed out at 4.35.*

Arrival	Name	Company	Visiting	Car reg	Departure
9.15	A. ZAHOS	PAPADOPOULOS	J. JONES	-	4.35
9.20	C. Wilson	-	Frank Gavin	-	9.25
9.20	P. Benson + G. Hall	OTIS	Operations	K938 PUF	-
9.30	Betty Khan	Marketing Horizons	Robert Vanek	.	9.55

Mr. Zahos / Jackie Jones 9.30 appt. Collected by Sarah de Souza (Marketing) Needs taxi 4.30!
Christina Wilson / FG. No appt. Coming back. Will make appt.
OTIS lift people. Lift No. 4 out of order. All day?
B. Khan / R. Vanek. Kept waiting 20 mins. RV didn't show up.
Left after complaint

2 Look at this extract from an Appointment Book and make statements using the words given.

e.g.: *Sue Lowe has an appointment with Alexis Thorne at 9 o'clock.*

have appointment with
see   need   replace   come

18 March		
Visitor	**Seeing**	**Comments**
Sue Lowe	Alexis Thorne 9.00	
Sally Wells	Jane Fox 9.00	car pass required
KJC Rep	John Burch 9.15	JB away. M. Bourne will see
LEX	collecting JR's car 10.00	Keys on desk

RECEPTION TRAINING AND THE RECEPTION AREA

KNOWING YOUR BUSINESS

Study the organisation chart of a typical company and check the departments you are not sure of. Study the enquiries and say which department in the organisation chart might be the most appropriate for each.

Enquiries

a I'd like to speak to the Sales Director, please.

b I'm enquiring about whether you have an office in Hong Kong.

c I'm phoning about your invoice no. 983370.

d I'm interested in doing work experience.

e Could you put me through to someone about confirming the rumour of the company merger?

f I am trying to trace a consignment that was sent by airmail.

g I'm calling on behalf of your German subsidiary. We haven't had the expense budget.

h I'm calling about the job vacancy in the paper.

i Can you put me through to someone who may be interested in an idea for a new project?

j I'm phoning about my October bill. It still hasn't been paid.

Organisation chart

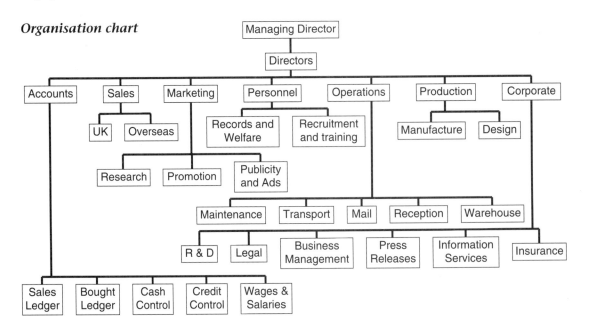

THE RECEPTIONIST'S EQUIPMENT

Study the following checklist of equipment and match the items with the functions. Are there any other items you would expect to have available at your desk, or in the reception area?

Equipment	Functions
a Visitor's Register	To find details of local services.
b Appointments Diary	To keep waiting visitors occupied.
c Staff List	For all visitors to sign in.
d Organisation Chart	For giving and taking messages.
e List of regular suppliers	To have all employees' names, depts. and nos.
f Health & Safety regulations and service nos.	To know who is expected.
g Telephone directory	To understand the company structure.
h Magazines and journals	For everyday stock and maintenance needs.
i Publicity literature	For enquiries about the company.
j Message forms	For quick reference in emergencies.

THE RECEPTION AREA

Study these pictures of reception areas.

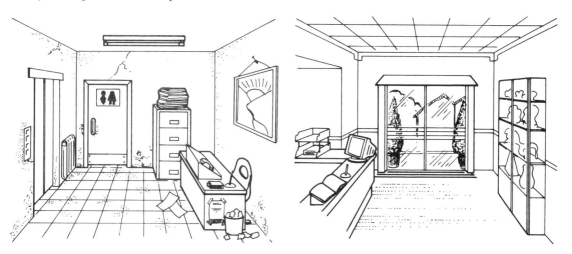

1 Match the words below with the appropriate parts of the pictures.

> switchboard   radiator   Visitor's Register   entrance   lift/elevator
> filing cabinet   filing tray   message pad   wastepaper basket
> display cabinet   cloakroom   Visual Display Unit (VDU)

2 What bad (or good) things can you say about these reception areas?

THE INTERNAL DIRECTORY

1 Study these extracts from two company internal directories (staff lists). If you had to use them, as a receptionist operating the switchboard, what problems would they cause you and how would you improve them?

Extract B ▶

December 1994

Allsop Y.	4567
Amberley D.	2367
Baker R.	1342
Bamforth K.	4658
Collin D.	3676
Davies L.	6555
Ellis W.	5643
Green H.	2367
Johnson E.	1209
Murray E.	4532
Mason J.	3268
Norton J.	1243
Personnel	5312
Taylor K.	2543

Extract A ▼

Finance		Sales	
3217	J. Bowles	2732	J. Allen
3220	D. Carter	2510	D. Smith
3242	F. Nolasco	2678	M. Harris
3217	B. Jackson	2458	D. Smith
3219	N. Knowles		
3206	S. Aslett		

2 List the features that you think constitute a good internal directory.

3 Study this extract from another internal directory. In which ways is it better? Look at the enquiries below and note which extension numbers you would contact or put the callers through to.

Enquiries

a I left the company last month and I still haven't had my final pay cheque.

b We want to know why our account is on hold.

c I am enquiring about a supplier invoice.

d I was wondering if your company would be interested in advertising in a new magazine.

e We are calling about the Press Release concerning the company acquisition.

f I've got the new security locks that were ordered.

g I've got a job interview at 2.30.

h Can I get hold of your products in the USA?

i Can you put me through to someone that can tell me the state of play on Model 463? It's supposed to be out tomorrow.

NAME		EXTN.	FLOOR	DEPT.	POSITION
Gregson	Janet	2578	2	Finance	Bought ledger clerk
Griffith	Tony	1543	1	Marketing	Publicity Officer
Ho	Susie	3689	G	Production	Production Controller
Hurst	Melanie	2368	2	Mgt. Inf.	Computer consultant
Keane	Karen	2529	2	Accounts	Credit Manager
Kelly	Tom	1488	1	Personnel	Personnel Manager
Le Bel	Nicole	3446	G	Finance	Payroll Controller
Nash	Angela	1432	1	Corporate	Managing Director
Neale	Harry	2987	2	Operations	Maintenance Officer
O'Neil	Jenny	1431	1	Corporate	PA to Angela Nash
Potter	Len	1321	1	Sales	Sales Manager Europe
Pratt	Marjorie	3211	2	Sales	Customer Services clerk

TALKING ABOUT RECEPTION

1 Read the following statements from receptionists talking about their work and answer the questions which follow.

A I like working in reception because you get to know a lot of people.

B I don't want to be a receptionist all my life, but it is a good way to start a career in business. You get to know all the departments and an overall view of the companies.

C I think, above all, you have to know how to keep cool and keep secrets! Keeping cool is not easy when the pressure is on and keeping secrets is fun!

D It gets a bit hectic, especially on Monday mornings, when you get loads of calls coming in and visitors all arriving for their 9 o'clock appointments.

E The worst thing is when you get people on the phone who don't seem to know who they want or what they want. It's not easy to decide who to put them through to.

F We have a separate switchboard, so my job is just to receive guests and direct them to their place of appointment.

G Well, we are such a small company, I have to do a whole range of things. I man the switchboard, I greet all the visitors, I make the tea and coffee … It's usually me that has to do the photocopying, I do the mail, I type Mr Hanson's letters … and guess who has the shoulder that everyone cries on or complains to!

   a Summarise the duties mentioned above, under positive and negative headings, according to the speakers' attitudes.

   b What do you think Speaker C means by 'keeping secrets'?

   c Find words in the speakers' statements which have the following meanings:

> *variety*   *correspondence*   *busy*   *calm*   *a lot of*   *connect*

2 ◁▭▷ Listen to some receptionists talking about their work and complete the chart.

	Duties	Likes	Dislikes
Speaker 1			
Speaker 2			
Speaker 3			

PART TWO

THE LANGUAGE OF RECEPTION: LISTENING AND UNDERSTANDING

UNIT 5   RECEIVING VISITORS

UNIT 6   TAKING MESSAGES AND BRIEF CALLS

UNIT 7   ENQUIRIES AND REQUESTS

UNIT 8   DEALING WITH PROBLEMS

RECEIVING VISITORS

1 ⬛ Listen to three situations. They are all exchanges between receptionists and visitors in a large international company. Complete the information in the chart.

	Appointment with	Time	Special Circumstances
a Mr Tanaka			
b Ms O'Connor			
c Mr Deleuse			

2   There were two clues telling us that Mr Tanaka had visited before. What were they?

3 ⬛ How did the receptionists express the following? Listen again, if necessary, and write their exact words.

  a   (*Conversation a*) She recognises her visitor ...

  b   (*Conversation a*) She will call Ms Lawson to let her know that her visitor has arrived ...

  c   (*Conversation b*) He enquires if he can be of assistance ...

  d   (*Conversation b*) He asks what the lady's name is ...

  e   (*Conversation c*) She asks the visitor to sit down ...

4 ⬛ Below are some of the expressions of the visitors. Complete the missing words. Listen again, if necessary.

  a   Mr Tanaka   *I am a ... early.*

  b   Ms O'Connor   *I am a ... late.*

  c   Mr Deleuse   *I ... an 11.15 committee meeting.*

Notes on usage and phraseology

I am	a bit	late
	little	early

an 11.15 meeting = a meeting at 11.15

Would you like to	take a seat?
	wait a while?
	wait a few minutes?
	wait a moment?

5 🔘 Listen to some more situations and answer the questions.

Situation A

a What does Ms Jordan want?

b Why can't she see the Personnel Manager?

c How does the receptionist help?

d Which expressions mean the following? Listen again, if necessary.
I need some help ...
Mrs Malin is not available ...
I will telephone her assistant ...
Sit down ...

Situation B

a Complete the sentences as you heard them:
May I ask if ... you?
So I can ... Mr Hawkins ... you are here.
I'll give his secretary ... to make sure he's ... .
Would you ... the book?
He's ... someone with him?

b In your opinion, did the receptionist handle this situation acceptably? Would you have acted differently?

c What expressions in the conversation mean the same as:

who do you work for?	wait	available
	coming	OK?

Notes on usage and phraseology

to expect someone = to know the person is coming

I presume he knows you = a polite way of saying *Does he know who you are?*

Would you mind + -ing? = please will you do it?

I've got a (Mr X) to see (Ms Y): Note the use of *a*. This is a slightly impersonal way of announcing someone who is probably not known, or expected.

on (her) way	down	
	up	= approaching
	over	

6 🔘 This time, you will hear several short statements or enquiries from visitors at a busy reception desk. Tick the correct category of visitor and note his/her requirements.

	With app.	Without app.	Postal delivery	Gen. Enquiry	Service Personnel	Temp staff	Job Applicant	Personal	Requirements
a									
b									
c									
d									
e									
f									
g									
h									
i									
j									

> **Notes on usage and phraseology**
>
> *to sign for something* = to acknowledge receipt in writing
>
> *I'm sorry to bother you, but* ... : A polite way of beginning a request
>
> *handy* = convenient
>
> *Look here* ... : A way of beginning a rather impolite complaint
>
> *on the off chance* = in the hope of (common introductory expression
> for people without appointments)

7 ▣ Study these questions and listen to the conversation.

    a What is the situation?
    b What is your opinion of the way the receptionist handles the visitor?
    c What can you say about the attitudes of the people?

8 ▣ True (✓) or false (✗)?

    a ☐ The receptionist is very efficient.

    b ☐ Mrs Janowski's appointment was for 11.20.

    c ☐ Mrs Janowski's husband is expected to phone her.

    d ☐ Kate Dodwell is not in.

    e ☐ Maggie is Tom Vincent's assistant.

    f ☐ The last caller probably had an enquiry about money.

9 ▣ Match expressions in the conversation with the following meanings. Listen again, if necessary.

    a Write your name in the book.
    b Of course.
    c There's something else.
    d He is not available.
    e The line is busy.
    f Do you wish to wait?
    g What is your name?
    h What is your request?
    i You will not have to wait long.
    j I have no idea.

10 Rewrite the situation following the same events, but make the receptionist more polite and helpful.

Mrs Janowski's request (see Mr Fish)

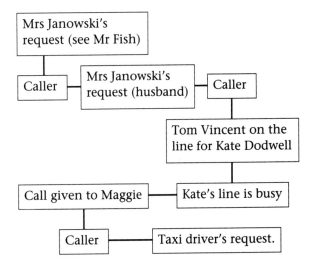

TAKING MESSAGES AND BRIEF CALLS

1 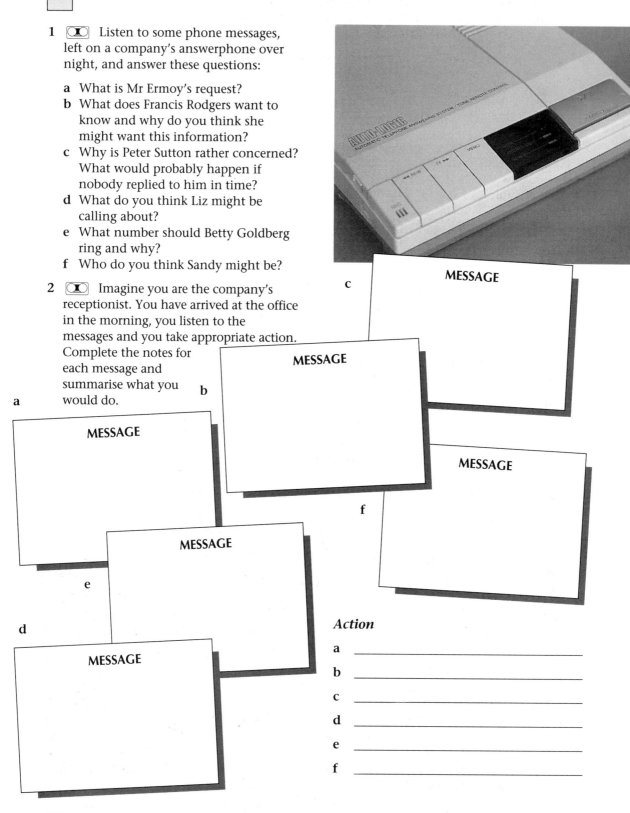 Listen to some phone messages, left on a company's answerphone over night, and answer these questions:

a What is Mr Ermoy's request?

b What does Francis Rodgers want to know and why do you think she might want this information?

c Why is Peter Sutton rather concerned? What would probably happen if nobody replied to him in time?

d What do you think Liz might be calling about?

e What number should Betty Goldberg ring and why?

f Who do you think Sandy might be?

2 Imagine you are the company's receptionist. You have arrived at the office in the morning, you listen to the messages and you take appropriate action. Complete the notes for each message and summarise what you would do.

a

MESSAGE

b

MESSAGE

c

MESSAGE

d

MESSAGE

e

MESSAGE

f

MESSAGE

Action

a _____

b _____

c _____

d _____

e _____

f _____

3 🔘 Imagine you are now passing these messages on to the appropriate people. Use your notes to reconstruct the messages. Work with a partner if possible.

4 🔘 Which expressions, in the recorded messages, have the same meaning as the following?

   a I will not be in the office.
   b Maybe she can telephone me so that we can arrange an alternative appointment.
   c It will not be possible for me to be there.
   d An unexpected incident has taken place.
   e Nobody will be here.
   f Is it possible for someone to return my call?

Notes on usage and phraseology

Ways of identifying yourself on the phone: This is ...
                                           My name is ...
                                         (Name) here

(I) won't be able to make	it	
	the meeting	= (I) can't come
	(tomorrow)'s meeting	

Something has come up =   common way of excusing yourself without specifying your reasons

reschedule = make another appointment

---

5 🔘 Sometimes, receptionists cannot put callers through to anyone and have to take notes of messages to pass on later. Listen to the callers' messages and study the receptionist's notes.
In each case, note what the receptionist did wrong and what he should have done.

a
> For R. Schmidt
> Helmut Janson
> called. Change of
> pick-up time. Now
> Tues 3rd @ 2 pm.

b
> For Gavin Costner
> (now in Sao Paulo?)
> Wife called.
> Not at home.
> Pls bring back
> C. Dior
> Tendre Poisson

c
> For David Martinez?
> (Universal) Sales?
> AWW – faulty batch
> of equipment

d
> For Mandy Gregg
> from Laura (Hong
> Kong). Paper
> time changed
> to 5/10 at 4.30.
> Jefferson Room
> Now on BA032
> leaving Manila
> at 19.05.
> Day early.

6 ⬤ Which expressions, in the messages you listened to, mean the following?

    a a person is unwell and not in the office
    b the request will be granted
    c if this doesn't happen
    d contact
    e please carry on, I am listening
    f would be equally acceptable

7 ⬤ Listen to some more brief messages and calls and choose the appropriate response to each, from the following:

☐ Of course not.

☐ May I ask who's calling?

☐ I think you have the wrong number.

☐ About 10 minutes by taxi

☐ I'm sorry. I'll try another extension.

☐ Yes. Where are you coming from?

☐ That's all right.

☐ Of course.

☐ I'll put you through to her assistant.

☐ I'm afraid not. Sorry. Not over the phone.

Notes on usage and phraseology

(I am) supposed to | (do)   = (I am) expected/required to (do)
               | (be doing)

get hold of = contact

take care of = handle/take responsibility for

(anyone) would do = (anyone) would satisfy the requirement

go ahead = continue

(I'm) calling on behalf of = representing

Have you got that? = Do you understand/ Is that clear?

Would you mind if ...? = Is it all right if ...?

ENQUIRIES AND REQUESTS

1 Listen to the calls received at the reception desk of different organisations and make notes of the calls below:

	Name of caller	Person/dept. requested	Nature of request
a			
b			
c			
d			
e			
f			
g			
h			
i			
j			

2 Listen to the calls again and make notes of your assessment of the situations and, particularly, of the way the receptionists handled them. Your notes should include:

- the different ways in which the receptionists answer the phone and what this implies about the receptionist and the organisation he/she works for.
- action taken/to be taken by the receptionist.
- details of how you would respond, if different.

3 Below are some of the receptionists' words from the situations you heard. Match the circumstances with the words.

Receptionists' words

I'll put you through to ...

Is it to do with ...?

He's fully booked.

Would 3 o'clock suit you?

Just call in any time.

As far as I know.

We don't have anyone by that name.

I'll see what I can do.

Circumstances

You can visit us when you like.

The receptionist checks that the time is acceptable.

The receptionist will do his/her best.

The receptionist is not 100% sure.

The receptionist will connect the caller to the person required.

The receptionist confirms that the person doesn't work in the building.

The receptionist enquires about the subject of the request.

The receptionist confirms that the person is not free.

4 Complete these sentences, taken from the situations you heard. Listen again, if necessary.

1 I have a question about the ... your models.
2 Could you possibly ... ?
3 You might ... trying.
4 Thank ... Scorpio.
5 Any ... ?
6 She could probably ... if you could ... .

Notes on usage and phraseology

Could you get me someone? = Could you find someone for me?

let someone know = inform someone

As far as I know = I am not 100% sure, but ...

We don't have anyone by that name = There is nobody here who has that name

Is it to do with ... ? = Does it concern ... ?/Is it connected with ... ?

I'll see what I can do = I will do my best to help

Would ... suit you? = Would ... be OK?

fully booked = no free time

She could probably fit you in = I think she will be able to see you

---

5 ☐🔊 Listen to the dialogue. There is a misunderstanding. Can you explain it? Can you spot other mistakes?

6 ☐🔊 Below are the responses given at a reception desk to some enquiries. Study them and see if you can guess what the types of enquiry are. Then listen to the enquiries and match them with the responses.

☐ *I'll enquire whether it has been reported.*　　☐ *Don't worry. I'll sort it out.*

☐ *No. She runs our Belgian operation.*　　☐ *I'll see that it's forwarded.*

☐ *He reports to Mrs Saunders.*　　☐ *They are seven hours ahead.*

☐ *I'm sorry. I didn't quite catch that.*　　☐ *I'll arrange for it to be collected.*

☐ *What is it in connection with?*　　☐ *I'm sorry I cut you off. I'll put you through again.*

☐ *I'll see if it's been handed in.*　　☐ *Would you like me to get her to call you back?*

Notes on usage and phraseology

Is that the right (office) to speak to ...? = Is that the correct place to speak to ...?

get hold of someone = contact someone

the line went dead = the telephone connection stopped

to be cut off = to have the telephone communication disconnected

someone who deals with ... = someone who works in ...

I'll enquire whether ... = I'll find out if ...

She runs our Belgian office = She is in charge of our Belgian office

He reports to ... = He is responsible to ...

I'm sorry. I didn't quite catch that = I did not understand/hear clearly

to hand something in = to leave something you have found, with someone (e.g. reception)

I'll sort it out = I'll see that it is done = I'll arrange for it to be done

get someone to call someone back = ask the person being called to return the call

DEALING WITH PROBLEMS

1 [▭] Listen to the extracts from a situation at the reception desk in an international company.

  a Who does Miss Gomez have an appointment with?
  b What is the problem?
  c What does Mrs Muller want?
  d What do you think is going to happen?

2 [▭] Which expressions in the listening in Exercise 1 indicate the following? Listen again, if you have to.

  a The person apologises for interrupting.
  b The person implies that there are not enough people working on reception.
  c The receptionist apologises about the other person waiting.
  d The person is getting very angry.
  e The receptionist apologises and explains the problem.

3 [▭] Listen to the continuation of the situation and summarise what has happened. What do you think will happen next?

4 [▭] Choose the correct response:

  a John Peters:
    i   is on the phone.
    ii is not in the office.
    iii doesn't wish to be disturbed.
  b Mrs Muller wants:
    i   to meet with Mr Peters tomorrow.
    ii to change the meeting to Friday.
    iii to confirm tomorrow's meeting with herself, Ruth Angelo and Mr Peters.
  c Maria Gomez:
    i   wants to see someone instead of Mr Peters.
    ii wants to be allowed to go straight to Mr Peters' office.
    iii wants to know who is in the office on the floor above Mr Peters.
  d The male caller is angry because:
    i   Alison Cooper's line is busy.

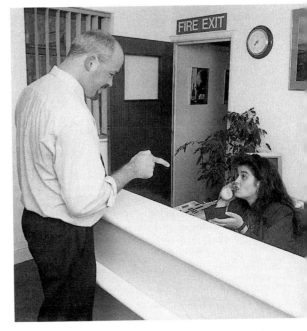

  ii he thinks the switchboard system is not good.
  iii he hasn't got any money.

5 [▭] Listen to the end of this situation and answer the questions.

  a What did the man with the parcel want?
  b How did the receptionist decide to help Miss Gomez?
  c What was Mr Bristow's problem?
  d What did Miss Gomez decide to do?
  e In your opinion, who is to blame for all this? Why?
  f Explain why 'Saved by the bell' might be an appropriate title for the situation.

6 [▭] Which of the receptionist's words from the situation match the functional situations below?

  a She says she is rather busy.
  b She has an idea which may help.
  c She is very sorry.
  d She says she has a caller for Alison.
  e She asks if the person will speak to the caller.

7 Complete the sentences below, taken from the situation, with the correct words.

else	way	nuisance	chance	afford	fact	ensure

a I don't want to be a ..., but about this parcel ...
b Are they for Mr Peters, by any ...?
c Isn't there anyone ... free?
d I will personally ... she gets the message.
e I can't ... to wait.
f And by the ..., that red Renault is mine.
g As a matter of ..., they are!

8 🔘 Choose responses below to match the statements and enquiries you hear.

☐ I'm afraid it's still engaged. Can you still hold, or would you like to call back later?

☐ I'm sorry. I'll remind them again for you.

☐ What seems to be the problem?

☐ Of course not. I fully understand.

☐ I'm terribly sorry to hear that. I'll notify the security guard.

☐ With it being the holiday period, we are a bit understaffed.

☐ I'll be with you just as soon as I can.

9 🔘 What are the people complaining about? Make a note of each complaint and where you would report it or direct the person to.

	Complaint	Report/direct to	
a		Sales Manager Customer Service Manager Production Manager	Personnel Manager Security Operations
b		Sales Manager Customer Service Manager Production Manager	Personnel Manager Security Operations
c		Sales Manager Customer Service Manager Production Manager	Personnel Manager Security Operations
d		Sales Manager Customer Service Manager Production Manager	Personnel Manager Security Operations
e		Sales Manager Customer Service Manager Production Manager	Personnel Manager Security Operations

PART THREE

THE LANGUAGE OF RECEPTION: LANGUAGE PRODUCTION

DEALING WITH VISITORS

1 Read the transcript of an exchange between a receptionist and a visitor and complete the summary information.

Name of visitor:

Position and Company:

Appointment with:

Time of appointment:

Notes:

Receptionist: Good morning.

Mr Santos: Good morning. I have an appointment with Ms Mason.

Receptionist: Right. Could I have your name, please?

Mr Santos: Santos.

Receptionist: I'm sorry. I didn't quite catch that. Could you repeat it, please?

Mr Santos: Santos ... Juan Santos.

Receptionist: And which company are you from?

Mr Santos: I'm the Sales Director at Candea in Barcelona.

Receptionist: May I ask the time of your appointment?

Mr Santos: Well, it was for 9 o'clock. I am sorry, I am rather late.

Receptionist: That's all right. If you'd like to sign in here, please, and take a seat, I'll just tell Ms Mason you have arrived.

Here's your visitor's badge. Could you just sign the book, please?

Mr Santos: Thank you. Could you tell me, er, is there somewhere I could leave this suitcase while I am in my meeting?

Receptionist: Yes, of course. If you'd like to leave it here, just by the desk, I'll keep my eye on it for you.

Mr Santos: Thank you. Oh, and I will need a taxi when I have finished the meeting. Would you be able to arrange that for me?

Receptionist: Yes. Just let me know when you are ready.

(A few minutes later)

Mr Santos: I'm sorry but Ms Mason hasn't in fact arrived herself yet. Her assistant will be down shortly. Would you mind explaining what it was that you were seeing Ms Mason about?

a Find expressions in the dialogue which are more polite ways of
saying the following:
Who are you?   Where do you work?   What time?   Sit down.
Someone will see you soon.   Why are you here?

b Use the cues below to make other polite statements and enquiries.
  i   May/ask/have/appointment?
  ii Could/give/name?
  iii Company/represent?
  iv Would/mind/sign in/Visitor's Register?
  v   Sorry/not catch/repeat?

c Using the following cues and the expressions from the dialogue,
reconstruct a similar dialogue. Work with a partner, if possible.

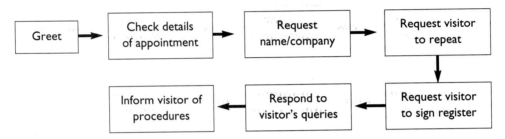

2 Match each statement or question on the left with the appropriate
response on the right.

Can I go up to Corporate?	Do you have an appointment?
I'm sorry I'm late.	Certainly.
I'm here for a meeting with John Hanks.	That's all right.
I've come to see the Production Controller.	How can we help you?
My name's Tanaka.	What time was it for?
I wonder if you could help me.	Are they expecting you?
I want to see the people in Accounts.	May I ask what it is about?

3 What would you say in these situations?

Situation   *Expression*
A visitor has been waiting a long time.
A visitor calls in on the off chance to see
  Mr Smith.
A visitor apologises for arriving early.
A caller has an order query.
A caller wants Mrs Howell but she is busy.
A visitor arrives for an appointment but
  doesn't remember who it is with.

4 Complete the chart with the words from the list.

Do you have an appointment?
It's nice to see you again.
Can I order you a taxi?
I'll let him know you are here.
Would you like to come this way?
Would you mind waiting a moment?
I am sorry. I don't know.
Can you find your way?
Hello. Can I help you?

Can I have your name, please?
Sorry to keep you waiting.
The ladies' room is over there, on the left.
Can I take your coat?
Can I get you anything?
Please take a seat.
I'll have a look for you.
I'm afraid she can't see you without an appointment.
She won't be a minute.

Apologising	Giving instructions

Offering help or service	Greeting

RECEPTION

Making enquiries	Giving information

5 Study the photographs below and the receptionists' comments on the next page. Match the comments with the photographs.

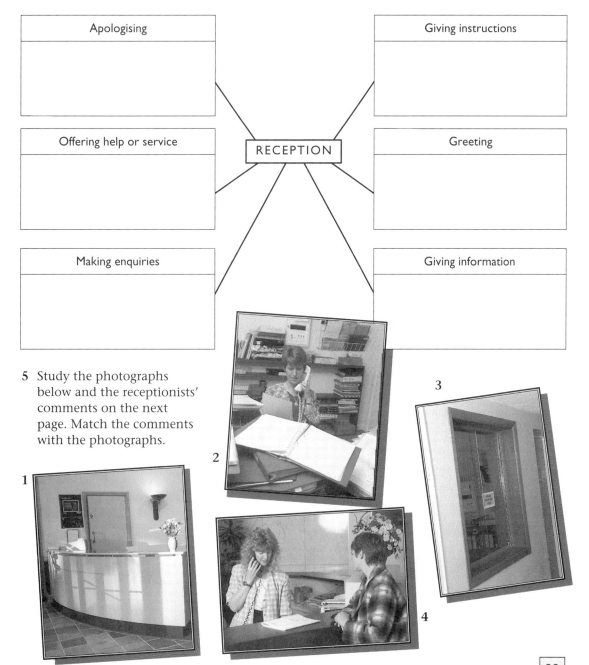

1

2

3

4

a It's ridiculous. There's far too much for one person to do. I have to look after the guests and operate an antiquated switchboard. On top of all that, they expect me to do the coffee and some of the typing!

b I am responsible for checking visitors in when they arrive. I find out who they are seeing, ring them up and direct them to the right floor. My office, if you can call it that, acts also as a security barrier, but there isn't a switchboard in there. There's no room for anything other than me and my phone directory!

c First thing in the afternoon is the worst. We start getting all the calls from the US. I'm usually on my own and for some reason, people seem to like that time for their appointments, so I often get queues building up between about 2 and 3.

d Our place is huge and very modern. My desk is quite discreet and uncluttered. It's more like a long table, really, with a vase of flowers. I don't have to deal with incoming calls at all. I just welcome the visitors.

6 Study the guests' exchanges with the receptionist and complete the conversations with what you think might be the receptionist's words.

a **Receptionist:** Good morning.
   Mr Hanbury: Good morning.
   Receptionist: ....?
   Mr Hanbury: I am here for a committee meeting at 12 o'clock.
   Receptionist: ....?
   Mr Hanbury: Hanbury. Jonathan Hanbury.
   Receptionist: ....?
   Mr Hanbury: I'm not sure. I think it was Jean Marsh's assistant.
   Receptionist: ....
   Mr Hanbury: Thank you.
   Receptionist: *(on phone)* ....?
      (to Mr Hanbury) ....
   Mr Hanbury: Thanks very much. By the way, where is Room 657?

b **Receptionist:** ....
   Ms Wu: Hello. My name's Karen Wu. I've come for an appointment with Frank Timms. It's for 3.45. I'm sorry, I am a little early.
   Receptionist: ....?
   Ms Wu: Sure ... Er, I am not sure of the car registration number. It's a hired vehicle.
   Receptionist: ....?
   Ms Wu: No thanks. I'll sit over there and read my notes.
   Receptionist: ....
   Ms Wu: Miss Relton? Who is that?
   Receptionist: ....
   Ms Wu: Oh, I see. Fine. Thank you.

c **Mr Bekesi:** Could you check upstairs again for me? I am just wondering if they have forgotten me.

Receptionist:	....
Mr Bekesi:	That's all right. It's not your fault.
Receptionist:	....?
Mr Bekesi:	That's right, but someone else in the Computer Room would do. It doesn't have to be Mike Weeks. The thing is, I have another appointment in an hour, so they'll have to hurry up.
Receptionist:	....?
Mr Bekesi:	Er, Bekesi, B-E-K-E-S-I. And it's not RJS Software, it's RJF Software.
Receptionist:	....
Mr Bekesi:	Thank you.

d

Mrs Othman:	I wonder if you could help me. I'm doing some research and would like the opportunity to ask some of your staff a few questions.
Receptionist:	....?
Mrs Othman:	No, I don't.
Receptionist:	....
Mrs Othman:	Well, it won't take more than a few minutes of their time.
Receptionist:	....?
Mrs Othman:	I'm not from a company. I'm a student.
Receptionist:	....
Mrs Othman:	Well, could I just sit down here and interview them as they go out?
Receptionist:	....
Mrs Othman:	The Personnel Department? All right, if you think that will help.

7 Rewrite the sentences using the words in brackets.

e.g. *Who are you? (May/have/name)* → *May I have your name?*

a What do you want? (How/help)

b It doesn't matter (Not worry/about/ that)

c Do you need anything while you are here? (Anything/get you/while/wait)

d I apologise for the delay (Sorry/keep/wait)

e Put your name in the book (Mind/fill details/ book?)

f You mustn't park there. Park in the multi-storey car park (Ask/you/not park/move/car/multi-storey)

g They will be here shortly (They/not be/minute)

h Are you sure about the way to Mr Zena's office? (Know/how/get/ Mr Zena/office)

i What about all those suitcases? (Like/leave/luggage/reception?)

j You can't see the Manager because you haven't got an appointment.(Afraid/manager/not available/without/appointment)

8 Match the two parts of these social exchanges:

Where are you from?	*Thank you.*
Your English is very good.	*Yes, I do.*
I would love to be able to speak a foreign language like that.	*Right in the centre of town.*
	I'm fine. And you?
Isn't it a horrible day today?	*For about five years.*
Is it cold outside?	*It's not bad.*
Where do you live exactly?	*From the north, originally.*
How long have you been with the company?	*If you live in the country you pick it up quickly.*
Do you like working here?	*Yes. Awful.*
How are you doing?	*It's not too bad. A bit chilly.*
What's it like over there?	

9 Practise the expressions using the models and cues below.

a *Would you mind filling* in the Visitor's Register?

fill in/Visitor's Register	wait there
take/seat	not smoke/reception area
leave/bags/reception	come back later
make/appointment	tell me/what about
speak more slowly	not push in

b *Could you tell me* who you are?

your name (Who?)	company name (What company?)
appointment time (What time?)	expected? (If?)
your business (What?)	duties (What/responsible?)
destination (Where?)	the name of the person (Who/speak to?)

10 Study the receptionists' memo pads and explain the situations. How would you convey this information to visitors.

a
VISITOR: PAULO GUALCO

Jeanette Bolton: supposed to be out of meeting by 12 noon. Ask Paul Qualco to wait. Suggest discussions over lunch.

b
Visitor: Mrs von Meijne

Personnel behind schedule with interviews. Mrs von Meijne rescheduled for 11.20. Apologise.

c
VISITOR: HEINRICH KNUCHEL

STRATEGY MEETING NOW IN JEREMY'S ROOM. SAME TIME. CAN COME UP. COFFEE BEING SERVED.

d
VISITOR: OFFICE SUPPLIES LTD

Work stations 2001 — 2050 in West Wing now ready for installation keys with Dorothy.

DIRECTING AND INSTRUCTING VISITORS

1 Study the expressions for directing visitors in an office or institutional building.

The					the	
	lift/elevator		next to			stairs
	stairs		opposite			hall
	canteen	is	behind			door
	toilets		just beyond			double doors
	post room		by			lift/elevator
	store room		round the back of			basement
	exit	are	on			first floor
	shop		up			top floor
	reception desk		down			corridor
	drinks machine		under			entrance
	telephone		along			exit
	photocopier		in front of			bridge
	conference room		across			steps
	escalator		inside			main doors
	fire escape		outside			passage
	library		near			
	main hall		through			
	(marketing) department		around			
	secretariat		at the end of			
			just past			
			above			
			facing			
			on the other side of			
			on your right			
			on your left			
			over there			
			between the ... and the ...			
			first (door) on your (right)			
			facing you			

I'm sorry.	There aren't isn't	any ... in the building a
	We don't have The nearest ... is ...	

You can't miss it
Carry straight on till you see ...

Common collocations

up/down the stairs	along the corridor/passage	over/under the bridge
across the hall	up/down the steps	through the doors
down the basement	through the entrance	around the corner
at the end of the corridor/passage		

2 Study the floor plans. Imagine you are at the reception desk, in each case, and answer the visitors' problems and questions, using the expressions on the previous page. Study the different ways the questions are formed.

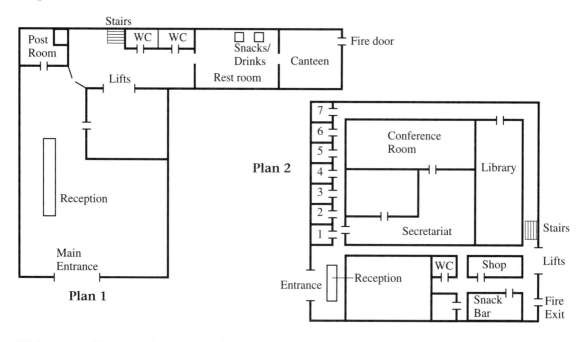

Plan 1

Plan 2

Visitors' problems and questions for Plan 1

a *Where are* the lifts?
b *Can you tell me if* there are any drinks machines?
c Excuse me, I can't find the stairs.
d *I'd like to know if* there is another way out.
e *Can I get* a photocopy of this done here?
f *I can't find* the loo!

Visitors' problems and questions for Plan 2

a *Is there anywhere where* I can get a sandwich or something?
b *Excuse me, whereabouts* is the conference room?
c *I was told* there was a small shop in the building. *Where exactly* is it?
d *Can you direct me to* Room 5?
e *Where can I find* the library?
f *How do I get to* the third floor?

3 Here are some common expressions made by receptionists. Can you
   guess the situations they refer to? Study the situations below and match
   them with the expressions to see how many you got right.

She won't be long now.

Follow me, please.

I can't recommend it personally, but a lot of our overseas staff stay there.

There's one on the corner.

It's yesterday's. OK?

Would you like me to order you one?

I haven't got any change. Sorry.

You'd better see someone in Operations.

Your best bet would be the chain store opposite.

You needn't be nervous. They're ever so nice.

Those are not for sale, I'm afraid.

I'm afraid you can't leave it there.

Nothing's been reported. I'll keep a look out.

No. This is number 342. Try further down.

Sorry. We couldn't get hold of you to let you know.

Who is it for?

Whereabouts are you going?

a You are going to escort the visitor to the meeting room.
b The visitor wants a chemist's.
c The visitor needs a taxi.
d The visitor is getting fed up with being kept waiting.
e The visitor asks for a newspaper.
f Someone has got the wrong building.
g The visitor has turned up for a meeting that has been cancelled.
h The visitor is enquiring about a nearby hotel.
i The visitor needs directions for getting out of town.
j The visitor has come for a job interview.
k Someone has come to offer a window cleaning service.
l Someone is handing over a package.
m The visitor is enquiring about a lost wallet.
n The visitor has parked her car where she shouldn't.
o The visitor enquires about buying one of the products in the display cabinet.
p The visitor wants to know where he can get a local map.
q The visitor wants some coins to make a phone call.

4 Rewrite the sentences using the words in brackets.

e.g. *Continue until you see the double doors, go through them and the toilets are by the stairs. (carry/past/find/next) Carry on past the double doors and you will find the toilets next to the stairs)*

a I think there is something missing. (look/like)
b I'm afraid you can't go up without an appointment. (unless)
c We need your number as we may have to telephone you about any alterations to the schedule. (in case/call back/changes/times)
d Unless you have parked in a reserved space, there shouldn't be a problem. (provided/OK)
e It is possible that someone found it and gave it to the security guard. (may have/hand in)
f I will ask someone to deliver it to you upstairs. (have/ send up)
g On leaving the lift, it is right opposite. (When/get out/see/facing)
h You'll find them behind the photocopier as far as you can go along the corridor. (located/round/back/end)
i You won't find shops in this area. (there/not/around here)

5 Study the delivery note below and answer the questions.

   a Who is it for?
   b Where has it come from?
   c When was it sent?
   d Who is the courier?
   e What are the contents?
   f How many packages?
   g What was the means of despatch?

6 Imagine you are calling the person to whom this package is addressed, to inform them of the delivery. Complete the sentences, using the words below.

Hello. This ... desk. A package ... you via ... from ... . I ... for it, and ... examined it. I think its the ... you've been waiting for.

SPEEDWAY
INTERNATIONAL EXPRESS

COURIER

C 9 4 7 0 7 6 4 5 6

DESTINATION	DATE	ORIGIN CODE
LONDON	5/10/95	

CONSIGNMENT NUMBER

C 947076456

SHIPPER'S ACCOUNT No.	CREDIT CARD/CHECK NO.	RECEIVER'S COMPANY NAME
046792		OAKTREE & CO

COMPANY NAME	FOR THE ATTENTION OF (NAME/DEPT)
LODDON AND LODDON LTD	KAREN ASHCROFT (MARKETING)

STREET ADDRESS	STREET ADDRESS
8-10 THE PARKWAY	147-149 THE LINKS
	CAMDEN TOWN

CITY	COUNTY/STATE	CITY	COUNTY/STATE
ANDOVER	HANTS	LONDON	

COUNTRY	ZIP CODE	COUNTRY	ZIP CODE
ENGLAND	SP47 8PU	ENGLAND	NW14 6RN

SENT BY (NAME/DEPT)	TELEPHONE NO.	RECEIVER	TELEPHONE NO.
JAMES COUSINS (ADVERTISING)	01264 947438	*Lucy Wilson* SIGNATURE	0181 465 920

CONTENTS	NO. OF PACKAGES	LUCY WILSON PRINT NAME	DATE	TIME
ARTWORK	1		6/10/95	9.35

OBSERVATION, EMERGENCIES, SECURITY AND INTERNAL STAFF MATTERS

1 List the expressions you know for describing people and their characteristics.

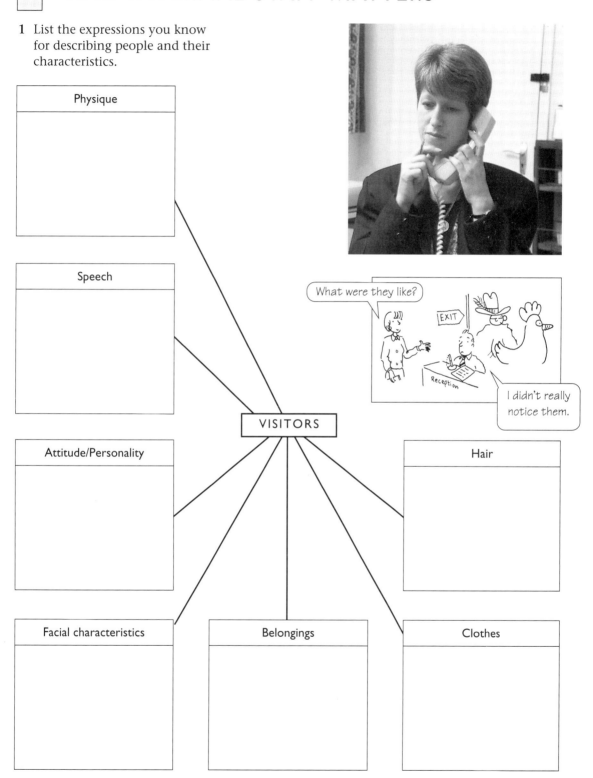

Physique

Speech

Attitude/Personality

Facial characteristics

VISITORS

What were they like?

I didn't really notice them.

Hair

Belongings

Clothes

2 Check which of these were on your list, look up those you don't know and add them to the chart on the previous page.

friendly	tall	curly	umbrella	moustache
arrogant	short	straight	briefcase	beard
shy	heavily-built	bald(ing)	carrier bag	glasses
cheerful	thin	long	box	square
serious	young	old	wavy	pony tail
nervous	good-looking	middle-aged	scruffy	smart
easy-going	plain	attractive	elegant	tee shirt
suit	jeans	shirt	blouse	skirt
overcoat	jacket	hat	fair	grey
loose-fitting	tight-fitting	quietly-spoken	loud	accent
charming	unpleasant	elderly	demanding	polite
(brown) eyes	made-up	tanned	pale	limp
talkative	vague	blunt	concise	impolite/rude
cool	sophisticated	sexy	(fair)haired	precise

Common collocations and expressions

She has (curly) hair	He is bald
He speaks with an accent	He looks scruffy
She has a square face	She has a pleasant personality
He is wearing a loose-fitting suit	She is quietly-spoken
He speaks with a (French) accent	In (his) (thirties)
(Straight) (black) hair	With (wavy)(red) hair
Dressed in ...	She was heavily made-up
With a pale face	What (was) (he) like? (Not: How was he?)
(She) walked with a limp	He is sort of ...

Note the order: An old, grey-haired and quietly-spoken man with glasses.
A polite young woman with a thin face and short hair, dressed in a grey skirt and carrying a red plastic bag.

3 Make *one* complete descriptive sentence from each of these notes.

    a man/pale/tall/American accent/briefcase/grey hair/glasses
    b woman/jeans/carrier bag/tight-fitting/curly/blonde
    c young man/smart/unpleasant/curly/wear/beard/suit
    d lady/grey/quietly-spoken/elderly/wavy

4 Study the people and describe each of them briefly.

Picture 1: _____

Picture 2: _____

Picture 3: _____

Picture 4: _____

Picture 5: _____

Picture 6: _____

5   Listen to some visitors talking and describe them below. Mention where you think the person might come from and what his/her attitude is like.

Speaker 1	Speaker 2	Speaker 3	Speaker 4	Speaker 5

6 Study the receptionists' expressions and match them with the situations.

  a *Attention please. Will all members of staff please leave the building immediately.*

  b *She just popped out.*

  c *I didn't have a chance to tell really. I think she had a foreign accent.*

  d *May I see your bag, please?*

  e *Try sipping this.*

  1 Security inspection

  2 Bomb or fire alert

  3 Offering a visitor or member of staff, who is unwell, a glass of water.

  4 Recalling a telephone caller's voice.

  5 Answering an enquiry about the whereabouts of a member of staff.

ON THE TELEPHONE

1 Study these message forms.

a

WHILE YOU WERE OUT   Date 25 July
To *Jack Hawkin*   Tel
Caller *Mrs Hawkin*   Time 10·15
☑ Please ring   ☐ No message
☐ Will call   ☐ Urgent
Message

Before 11 am.

b

WHILE YOU WERE OUT   Date 4 February
To *Mary Wilson*   Tel 512370
Caller *Jane (Apex Recruitment)*   Time 11·0
☑ Please ring   ☐ No message
☐ Will call   ☐ Urgent
Message

wants to know if we have any vacancies that need filling

c

WHILE YOU WERE OUT   Date 8 March
To *Jon Petrie*   Tel
Caller *SKANDECOR*   Time 4·20
☐ Please ring   ☐ No message
☑ Will call   ☐ Urgent
Message

Are we interested in purchasing office furniture? Didn't catch name.

d

WHILE YOU WERE OUT   Date 12 April
To *Joan Thomas*   Tel ext. 290
Caller *Jackie (Personnel)*   Time
☐ Please ring   ☐ No message
☐ Will call   ☑ Urgent
Message

Snag with Management course next week. I dropped out. Replacement?

e

WHILE YOU WERE OUT   Date 19 May
To *Mike Cragg*   Tel 33147063711
Caller *Penny Tranter*   Time 2·35
☑ Please ring   ☐ No message
☐ Will call   ☐ Urgent
Message

State of play/latest news on production schedule. June 17 visit OK?

f

WHILE YOU WERE OUT   Date 21 April
To *Pauline Lawrence*   Tel
Caller *Hans Meyer*   Time 11·50
☐ Please ring   ☑ No message
☐ Will call   ☐ Urgent
Message

Didn't leave message or number.

2 Report the information in the message forms to the people for whom the messages were taken.

e.g.

a Mr Hawkin? This is Leila on reception. There was a message from your

wife at 10.15. Please can you call her before 11 o'clock?

_____

_____

b _____

_____

_____

_____

c _____

_____

_____

_____

d _____

_____

_____

_____

e _____

_____

_____

_____

f _____

_____

_____

_____

3 Note the ways of reporting these messages. Practise the expressions, substituting other details of your own.

... will call again	I've got a message from ...
There's a snag/problem with ...	... called to enquire if/whether/about
Is that ...?	... called from ...
... would like you to ...	.... wants to know if we would be interested in ...
... asked if you would call	... didn't leave a message

4 Below are written extracts from telephone messages. Report each message as shown in the example. Study the **Notes on usage and phraseology** if you need help.

> E.g. *Harry Green: I won't be able to make the Tuesday meeting. (call)*
> → *Harry Green called to say he wouldn't be able to make the Tuesday meeting.*

a Felicity Worsley: I shall be in late today. (call)
b Greg Johns: Can she call me please, as soon as possible? (ask)
c Kate Fleming: I saw the overseas reps after all. (phone)
d Emiko: Let me know if you can keep the first week in August free. (want to know)
e Jan Laarsson: I'll be arriving on Wednesday 5 at about 2 o'clock. (say)
f Tulin Aksu: When is the sales meeting rescheduled for? (want to know)
g Eric Hutson: I will send the report in two days. (promise)
h Tina Poulos: Can someone send me an updated price list? (wonder)
i Nancy Baker: I didn't manage to see Harumi. (call)
j Hank O'Keefe: Don't forget to bring some disks. (want to make sure)

Notes on usage and phraseology

I look forward to it.	→ He *says* he *looks* forward to it.
	→ He *said* he *looked* forward to it.
Do you smoke?	→ She *asked if/whether I smoked.*
	She *wants to know if/whether smoke.*
Have you met Mrs Danton?	→ He *wondered if/whether* I *had* met Mrs Danton.
Where *can we* meet?	→ She *asked where we could* meet.

NB Yes/No questions are reported with *if* or *whether*

In reported questions, the word order is not like a question and the question mark disappears.

After a reporting verb in the past tense, the other verbs in the sentence usually change, e.g.

It is	→ He said it was.
They will	→ He said they would.

5 Use the words in the box to report the messages and queries. The words can be used more than once and there are sometimes different possibilities for each. Study the **Notes on usage and phraseology** if you need help.

> e.g. *She asked when the Accounts Department closed.*
> *He enquired about the closing time of the Accounts Department.*

tell	*say*	*ask*	*complain*	*wonder*	*request*	*suggest*

  a What time does the Accounts Department close?
  b Please call me back after 4 o'clock.
  c He hasn't even replied to my last two letters.
  d I am puzzled. Why don't you spend more on promotion?
  e It would be a good idea to drop Marcus Grainger a line.
  f I shall leave after lunch.
  g Is Charles in today?
  h How are sales doing?
  i Please tell Wendy Jones that she shouldn't worry about the presentation. I'll have it ready by tonight, if she'd like to call me.
  j I would like the overseas address of Jana Masson.

Notes on usage and phraseology

tell someone *to do* something/*not to do* something
complain that + noun + verb (e.g. She complained that they were late.)
complain about + noun (e.g. She complained about the delay.)
wonder if/whether/when/why/what/who
request someone *to do* something
request that + noun + verb (e.g. I request that she comes immediately.)
suggest + noun + verb (e.g. I suggest you call her.)
suggest that + noun + verb (e.g. I suggest that you call her.)

---

6 Rewrite the sentences using the words in brackets.

> e.g. *He was complaining about the service (that/bad)*
> → *He was complaining that the service was bad*

  a He said 'Don't be late.' (tell/you)
  b If I were you, I would ignore it. (suggest)
  c He requested that you should phone him. (ask/call back)
  d They said they would be here shortly. (not be long)
  e She said she would send a fax. (reply)
  f He asked if the modems were compatible. (wonder/whether)

7 Match the appropriate telephone responses with the situations.

a Who was it you were calling?

b Can you hold?

c I'll put you through to her assistant.

d I am not sure. Would you like me to find out?

e He didn't say.

f Sorry. The line's still engaged.

g I'll try again for you.

h I'll see if I can find her.

i He's tied up at the moment. Can I get him to call you back?

j Where are you calling from?

Situations

1 The receptionist doesn't know where the person required is, but will try to locate her.
2 The person required is very busy. The receptionist enquires if the caller would like this person to phone when he is free.
3 The person required is talking on the phone.
4 The receptionist wants to know if the person is prepared to wait.
5 The receptionist checks the name of the person required.
6 The receptionist wants to know the caller's location.
7 The receptionist doesn't know the answer to the caller's question but offers to help.
8 The information requested is not available.
9 The person required was unavailable, but the receptionist offers to put the caller through to an assistant.
10 The receptionist offers to connect the person a second time.

8 Match the receptionists' responses to the callers' statements or queries and note how the receptionists deal with each case.

Caller

a I'd like some information.
b Can you put me through to someone who can help me with an enquiry?
c Is Joanna available, please?
d I want to speak to the manager. They said she is still busy. Can you interrupt her, please, or intercept the conversation if she is on the phone?
e Hi. This is Martin, from upstairs. I've got Jack Foster in my office. He's not feeling at all well. I'm not sure what to do.

Receptionist

☐ *We have several people with that name. Do you know her other name?*

☐ *Who's calling please? I'll ask his secretary.*

☐ *Your first-aid officer on that floor is Mary Fletcher, but I can call a doctor, if you like.*

☐ *What kind of information?*

☐ *Can you give me some more details?*

9 **a** Which of the following expressions are likely to be particularly for telephone communication?

b Suggest situations for each expression.

c Which expressions do you think you should avoid using? Suggest some correct equivalents.

Expressions

Hang on.	*Would you mind removing it?*
Where are you from?	*Can you call back later?*
Please wait a moment.	*I'll make a note of it.*
Can I get you something to drink?	*I have Ms Rodrigues on the line.*
Hold the line please.	*Sorry to keep you waiting.*
Putting you through.	*Just a minute.*
Okey dokey.	*Who's calling?*
The line's engaged.	*I'm afraid I must ask you to leave.*
Will you hold?	*Ta ta.*
Can you spell that?	*May I have your number?*
See you.	*What is it about?*
Sorry, dunno.	*Can I take your coat?*
Would you like me to call you one?	*I'll try another extension.*
Would the driver of vehicle registration	*What?*
number ... please come to reception?	*What company are you from?*
Are you trying to sell us something?	*Sorry, you can't smoke here.*
I can't understand a word you're saying.	*I'll enquire whether anyone has seen it/them.*
Would you like to take a seat?	*Mr Turner won't be a minute.*

PART FOUR

REFERENCE

TAPESCRIPT

USEFUL PHRASES

ANSWER KEY

TAPESCRIPT

Exercise 2

Speaker 1: The thing I like the least is the monotony of answering the phone, especially as I am on my own behind my little window all day long. Apart from that, I am responsible for telling staff when their visitors arrive. That's OK because at least you make contact with people.

Speaker 2: There is face to face contact with people, of course – which is a plus – but it's usually so busy that there's not much time to really communicate with anyone, which I find frustrating. Basically, I share taking the incoming calls – that involves putting callers through to the right person – and I tell people when their visitors arrive. Oh, and I get them to sign the book, of course, which is our record of who is coming and going in the place. Very occasionally, I get the chance to talk to some of the visitors, like when they are kept waiting, or they've come early, or need help with something. I enjoy that.

Speaker 3: The worst thing about my job is when people in the company don't answer their phones and can't be found. There's a lot of them like that ... It really is annoying, when you've got an impatient person on the line and the others are queuing up. We have a new system of recorded messages on individual extensions which people can programme onto their phones when they're away from their desk. But callers often don't want this. They'd prefer to speak to someone else. And then, when they don't have a name, it's a question of trying to assess who the best alternative person would be. It's not easy!

UNIT 5

Exercises 1 – 4

a Mr Tanaka:	Good afternoon. My name is Mr Tanaka. I have a 2.30 appointment with Ms Lawson. I am a little early ... Could you remind me where the men's room is?	
Receptionist:	Of course. Hello Mr Tanaka. It's nice to see you again. I'll let Ms Lawson know you are here. The men's room is on the first floor, on the left of the lifts.	
b Receptionist:	Good morning. Can I help you?	
Ms O'Connor:	Yes. Good morning. I am supposed to see Brigitte Meyer at 10.30. I'm a bit late, I'm afraid.	
Receptionist:	Could I have your name, please?	
Ms O'Connor:	O'Connor. Rachel O'Connor.	
c Mr Deleuse:	Hello. I'm Alain Deleuse. I have come for an 11.15 committee meeting, but I am not sure of the name of the person who organised it.	

Receptionist:	That's all right. Let's see what we can do ... Do you know the name of the committee?
Mr Deleuse:	Yes. It's the East European Policy Steering Committee.
Receptionist:	Oh yes, I see. You'll be in Conference Room B and it's being organised by Jim Hanks. Would you like to take a seat and I'll tell them you're here.

Exercise 5

Situation A

Receptionist:	Hello there.
Ms Jordan:	Good afternoon. I wonder if you could help me? I'd like to see your Personnel Manager please.
Receptionist:	Do you have an appointment?
Ms Jordan:	Well, no. Actually I don't. But I'd like some more information about the vacancy advertised for a marketing assistant.
Receptionist:	Mrs Malin isn't normally able to see people without an appointment and, in any case, she's not in this afternoon. But I'll tell you what I will do. I'll give her assistant a call and see if she will be able to have a word with you. She might at least be able to give you some job details and maybe you could then make an appointment.
Ms Jordan:	Oh, that's very kind of you. Thank you.
Receptionist:	Have a seat while I try for you. May I have your name?
Ms Jordan:	It's Kathy Jordan

Situation B

Receptionist:	Excuse me, sir. Can I help you?
Mr Gordon:	What? No thank you. I'm going to see Charles Hawkins. Fourth floor isn't it?
Receptionist:	May I ask if he is expecting you?
Mr Gordon:	Expecting me? He might be. I'm not sure.
Receptionist:	Can I have your name, sir?
Mr Gordon:	I don't really see why. It doesn't really matter ...
Receptionist:	So I can let Mr Hawkins know you are here.
Mr Gordon:	Oh, very well. I'm Arthur Gordon.
Receptionist:	Which company are you from Mr Gordon?
Mr Gordon:	Company? I'm not from any company.
Receptionist:	I presume Mr Hawkins knows you, Mr Gordon?
Mr Gordon:	I should say so! We were out together last night. That's why I am here. He's still got my car keys!
Receptionist:	Oh, I see. Well, if you'd like to hold on a moment, sir, I'll give his secretary a call, to make sure he's around. Would you mind signing the book while I do that? And here's a Visitor's Badge.

Mr Gordon:	This all seems rather unnecessary, but all right, if I must ...
Receptionist:	Hello, Pam? It's Jeanette. I've got a Mr Gordon to see Charles ... . He says he's got his car keys ... He's got someone with him? ...Well, can I send him up? Maybe you can help ... Oh, all right.
(Pause)	Mr Gordon? ... Mr Hawkins is in a meeting at the moment, but his secretary is on her way down to attend to you. All right?

Exercise 6

a Male:	Express Parcels. Can you sign for this, here please? Cheers.
b Male:	I'm a close friend of Mary Salina. Could you let her know that I'm here. Just say that Jethro is in Reception.
c Female:	I'm sorry to bother you, but do you have any aspirins here? I'm in the sales meeting upstairs and I've got a terrible headache.
d Female:	Hi. The meeting finished early, so I've got some time to spare. Could you tell me if there are any gift shops around here?
e Male:	Morning. Sunbright. We are here to clean the inside windows.
f Female:	Hello. I'm Dominique Lafon. I start here this morning for a two week temporary job. I was told to report to ... er ... Mrs Angelica?
g Male:	Good afternoon. I've come to fix Mrs Daly's computer. Is there anywhere I can leave the van that's handy for loading and unloading?
h Female:	Look here, I've been waiting here for over half an hour and nobody's come to collect me. Isn't there anything you can do about it? It's disgraceful. My appointment was for 11.30.
i Male:	I've come on the off chance of seeing someone in your marketing department. I'm a freelance designer.
j Female:	Hello. I'm Jane Forster. I'm a bit late, I'm afraid. I've come for a job interview with ... er ... Mr Schrand.

Exercises 7–10

Receptionist:	... I know, it's awful isn't it? ... Really? ... Listen, I must go, I've got someone waiting ... OK ... Yes, of course ... See you tonight. Bye.
Mrs Janowski:	Hello. My name is Mrs Janowski. I've got a meeting with George Fish at 11.15.
Receptionist:	OK. Sign the register while I tell Mr Fish that you are here. *(Phone rings)* IBS, good morning ... Certainly.

Mrs Janowski:	And there's one other thing … My husband … *(Phone rings)*
Receptionist:	IBS, good morning … I'm sorry, he's not in today … Yes, she is … I'm putting you through …
Mrs Janowski:	My husband may call about collecting me. If he does, could you put him through or tell him … *(Phone rings)*
Receptionist:	IBS, good morning … I'll try for you … The line's engaged. Will you hold? … Yes. Who's calling? … One moment please … Maggie? I've got Tom Vincent for Kate … Thanks … Hello, Mr Vincent? I'm putting you through to Mrs Dodwell's assistant … Right, now, what was it you wanted?
Mrs Janowski:	I said if my husband calls, could you put him though to me or give him a message?
Receptionist:	Could you give me your name again?
Mrs Janowski:	Janowski …
Receptionist:	And you're seeing …
Mrs Janowski:	Mr Fish.
Receptionist:	Oh yes. Did you sign the book?
Mrs Janowski:	Not yet. Is there a pen handy?
Receptionist:	Don't you have one? Hold on … *(Phone rings)* IBS, good morning … Er, can you tell me what it's to do with? … Yes … Well, I'll try Accounts for you …
Taxi driver:	Excuse me.
Receptionist:	Yes, can I help you?
Taxi driver:	Taxi to collect someone for the airport.
Receptionist:	Hi. Hold on … Hello? Hold the line … Yes, I know, but we're very busy. I won't keep you a moment … God, some people are so rude! I've got a good mind to cut him off … Right! Who is the taxi for?
Taxi driver:	Don't ask me. They just said to be here at 11.20 to take someone to the airport … And it's already half past.
Receptionist:	That's a lot of help, I must say. Hold on …
Mrs Janowski:	Look here …

UNIT 6

Exercises 1–4

a Male:	Er, hello. This is Patrick Ermoy … That's E-R-M-O-Y. I'm leaving a message for Ruth Atkins in your Production Department … It's to say that I won't be able to make tomorrow's meeting … Something has come up … er. Sorry … Perhaps she could call me to reschedule.

b	Female:	Good evening ... Can I speak to ...? er ... sorry ... er ... My name is Francis Rodgers ... That's Rodgers with an 's' ... My number is 3468754. I want to know if you have an office or agency ... or branch ... or whatever you call it ... in Brussels. Could someone call me back please? Thanks. Bye.
c	Male:	Oh, hello. Peter Sutton here ... Area Sales Manager for Eastern Europe. I'd like to leave a message for Debbie Dickinson. Please inform her that I really must have a reply tomorrow ... that's Friday 20th ... to my faxes about her visit. This is very urgent as there won't be anyone around after tomorrow to take any calls. She has my number. Thank you.
d	Female:	Hi. Liz Saunders here. Dolphin Design. Message for Shireen or Joe in Advertising. Please call tomorrow before 10.
e	Male:	This is Premier Travel. Robert Day speaking. Please inform Betty Goldberg that her air ticket to Geneva will be ready for her at the Swiss Air desk from eight onwards tomorrow morning. If there's any problem, she can call me on 0171 794 5643. Goodbye.
f	Female:	Hello. This is Sandy from Credit Control. Please let Penny know that I'm very sorry but I won't be in tomorrow. I've got a bad upset stomach. I should be OK and back in the office on Monday.

Exercises 5 and 6

a	Male:	Can I leave an important message for Richard Schmidt, please?
	Receptionist:	Yes, go ahead.
	Male:	OK. This is his friend, Helmut Janssen. I'm supposed to be picking him up on Wednesday 3rd at 2 and I have to change this to Tuesday 2nd at 3. Bye.
b	Female:	Hello. This is Gavin Costner's wife. I know he's not in the office at the moment because he's still in Saõ Paulo, but I can't get hold of him there and his assistant is off sick today. Could I leave a message for him with you? Maybe you could find someone who knows exactly where he is.
	Receptionist:	Sure. I'll take care of it for you. What's the message?
	Female:	Right, well there are two messages. First, I am not at home for the next few days, but I can be contacted at Jana's. He knows the number. And second, could he bring back a bottle of Christian Dior Tendre Poison? That's the Eau de Toilette, by the way. OK? Thanks.
c	Male:	Good afternoon. Is that the same company as Universal?
	Receptionist:	Yes, we are the same. The two companies recently merged.

Male:	Right. Well I'm trying to get hold of a David Martinez, who used to be with Universal.
Receptionist:	Well, we haven't got all the names yet. Not everyone has moved in from Universal.
Male:	OK, well, if you could take the message, I'd be grateful. Mr Martinez was in the Sales Division, so if ever you can't get him, I suppose any senior sales person would do. I'm calling on behalf of AWW. We've just supplied Universal with some equipment and it is important for someone to know pretty quickly that the last batch is faulty and needs replacing. It shouldn't be used at all. All right? Have you got that?
Receptionist:	Yes. I'll try and find Mr Martinez and if all fails, I'll make sure the Sales Director knows immediately.
Male:	Thanks. Goodbye.
d Female:	Oh, hello there. This is Laura from the convention office in Hong Kong. I need to get an urgent message through to Mandy Gregg, but I understand she's not in today.
Receptionist:	Well, I can probably ensure she gets the message, if you'd like to leave it with me.
Female:	OK. Well, there are two things. The time of Ms Gregg's paper has been changed. She's now talking on October 5 at 4.30 in the Jefferson Room. Now, this means she'll have to get here a day earlier, so I've arranged for her flight from Manila to be changed. She's now on the BA032 which leaves Manila at 19.05. And the other part of the message is that there won't be any video facilities in the room. Can I leave all that with you?
Receptionist:	Yes, of course.

Exercise 7

a Female:	Hello. Can you tell Gerry Watkins that I will be half an hour late, please?
b Male:	Would you mind if I left an urgent message with you, for one of the staff?
c Female:	I'm doing some research for a study project. Can you tell me the approximate number of employees in the building?
d Male:	Can you put me through to your Managing Director, please?
e Female:	Excuse me, do you have a Winston Sommerville working for you?
f Male:	Can you give me directions how to reach your offices?
g Female:	How long does it take to get to your premises from the station?

h	**Male:**	I'm sorry to bother you.
i	**Female:**	Hello darling. I just wanted to say how much I shall miss you.
j	**Male:**	It's me again. You put me through, but there was no reply, so I had to call again. I have to speak to someone about this matter!

UNIT 7

Exercises 1–4

a	**Receptionist:**	Good morning, GAPCO.
	Male:	Hello. My name is Wertz. Helmut Wertz. Could you get me someone in the sales or customer service department please? I have a question about the availability of one of your models.
	Receptionist:	I'll put you through to Anne Bishop in the Sales Department.
b	**Receptionist:**	Hoskins, good afternoon.
	Female:	Hello? I have an appointment today at 2 o'clock, with Geoffrey Palmer. I will be a little late. My name is Sophie Boyard.
	Receptionist :	I'll try Mr Palmer's office for you.
	Female:	Er, I am in a terrible hurry and have no more coins for the phone. Could you possibly let them know?
c	**Receptionist:**	Hello. Express Graphics.
	Male:	Good morning. I am seeing Ms Jackson tomorrow. Could you fax me a map or something, so I can see exactly how to reach you? I'm coming by car.
	Receptionist:	Yes, I'll arrange that for you. Do we have your number?
d	**Receptionist:**	Computer Doctor. Jane speaking. How can I help you?
	Female:	Hi there. Georgina, please.
	Receptionist:	I am sorry, as far as I know, we don't have anyone by that name. Is it to do with repairing a computer?
e	**Receptionist:**	Grantley Books. Good morning.
	Male:	Could you please put me through to someone who can help me with an enquiry about the possibility of a work training attachment?
	Receptionist:	I'll see what I can do.
f	**Receptionist:**	Concorde.
	Female:	I asked for Brian Bradfield a few moments ago, but there was no reply. Can you try and put me through to his assistant, or someone in that department?
	Receptionist:	They are always busy in that department. I'll try for you, but you might just have to keep trying.
g	**Receptionist:**	Hi there. Thank you for calling Scorpio. How can I help you?

Male:	My name's Christos Pantos. I am a free lance artist. I would like to call in to see the Head of your Design Department. Could you give me his or her name and put me through to someone so I can make an appointment ?
Receptionist:	Well, her name is Judy Thompson and I don't really think you need to make an appointment. Just call in any time. They're on the fifth floor.

h

Receptionist:	The Hair Shop. Hello?
Female:	Hello. This is Fiona Earle here. I'd like to make an appointment with Carla, for a haircut and highlights, please.
Receptionist:	Any particular time?
Female:	Could she see me on Wednesday?
Receptionist:	Would 3 o'clock suit you?
Female:	That would be fine.

i

Receptionist:	Surgery.
Male:	Hello. I'd like to see Dr Talbot please.
Receptionist:	He's fully booked until Thursday, I'm afraid.
Male:	Oh dear. It can't really wait till then. It's not an emergency, but I wouldn't like to leave it till Thursday.
Receptionist:	Well, he could probably fit you in if you could get here straight away ...

j

Receptionist:	Bell Conference Centre. Good evening.
Female:	Good evening. Could you try and put me through to my husband, please? He's attending a conference at the moment.
Receptionist:	Of course. Can I have the name, please?
Female:	George Hanson. He's with the Apex group.
Receptionist:	Er ... they haven't come out yet. Can I take a message?

Exercise 5

Receptionist:	Sun Media. Can I help you?
Male:	Oh yes, hello. Chris Chang please.
Receptionist:	Just a minute ... Hello? I am sorry, but Mr Chang is not in office today. He is in Korea until tomorrow. Please can I help you?
Male:	This is his colleague, Mike Lister from the UK office. Listen, when he gets back from Korea, ...
Receptionist:	Tomorrow. He get back tomorrow.
Male:	Yes I know ... but *when* he returns, please tell him to ring me ...

Exercise 6

a Is that the right office to speak to Jose van Lennep?

b It's Mandy in R&D. I forgot to tell Mr Holton yesterday, that I wouldn't be in today and I can't get hold of him now.

c We just sent some mail for Henri Martini to your office address, but we hear he's been moved to another branch.

d Hi. It's Karen from upstairs. Can you get me a number in Indonesia, please? What time is it there?

e It's Jeanette Dabo again. I asked to speak to Sandy Aston and then the line went dead.

f A dog has just run through my office. Can you check it out?

g Who is Peter Young's boss?

h My company car is due for a service tomorrow, but I won't be able to take it in myself. Can you help?

i Hello. This is Tony Harper from Sales. I want to speak to Clementine Chartier but no one can find her. I'm phoning from my hotel in Tokyo.

j I left a green plastic carrier bag with some books and catalogues in it, when I called in yesterday. Can you help?

k I'd like to speak to someone who deals with promotion.

l (Very bad line, so speech is unintelligible) Hello? This is Gertrude Obermeyer speaking, from Munich. Can you put me through to ...?

UNIT 8

Exercises 1–2

Receptionist:	Good morning, GKK Ltd.
Caller:	Hello. Alison Cooper please.
Receptionist:	Thank you.
Miss Gomez:	Sorry to bother you again, but no one has come down for me yet. Could you check John Peters' extension again? My appointment was for 11.15.
Receptionist:	Yes, of course. I'm sorry you're being kept waiting, Miss Gomez.
	(phone)
	Excuse me a moment. Good morning, GKK Ltd.
Mrs Muller:	Look here! I've been trying to get through for ages. Are you understaffed or something?
Receptionist:	I'm awfully sorry. The thing is, the lines are very busy at the moment. Who was it you wanted?
Mrs Muller:	John Peters.

Exercises 3 and 4

Receptionist:	I'm terribly sorry, but both John Peters' lines are engaged. Can you hold, or is there someone else I can try for you?
Mrs Muller:	This is ridiculous! Listen, this is a matter of some urgency. Can you see to it that Mr Peters is informed that the meeting scheduled for tomorrow, with myself and Ruth Angelo, has been moved to Friday, because Mrs Angelo can't make it tomorrow. Same time, same place.
Receptionist:	And you are ...?

Mrs Muller:	Mrs Muller.
Receptionist:	And can I have your number, Mrs Muller?
Mrs Muller:	He knows my number.
Receptionist:	Oh dear ... As you probably heard, Miss Gomez, Mr Peters' line is engaged ... I am afraid you'll still have to wait till I get through.
Miss Gomez:	This really isn't good enough. Can't you tell someone else in his department that I'm here? Can't I just go on up? Who's above him? I've got a good mind to speak to his boss.
Receptionist:	I'll just try another number for you. *(phone)* I'm sorry ... Good morning, GKK Ltd.
Caller:	I phoned a few minutes ago, for Alison Cooper. There was no reply and I was just left waiting. No sound, no nothing, so I have had to call again. Isn't there some way you people can get back to callers, or try another number, instead of just leaving people stranded? It costs money to keep calling, you know.

Exercises 5–7

Receptionist:	I do apologise. I'll try again for you and if there's no reply, I'll put you through to her assistant ... Hello? I've got someone on the line for Alison ... She's not? Oh dear. Well, can you take the call please? ... Well, isn't there anyone else free? ... Hello, caller? ...I'm afraid I've not had much success. Ms Cooper is not in today and her assistant is in a meeting. All I can suggest is you call back or give me your name and number and I will personally ensure she gets the message ... Hello? ... Hello? ... Oh dear, he's gone. I hope I didn't cut him off ... Now, Miss Gomez, I'll try that number for you ...
Courier:	Hello there. Express package for Mr Peters to sign for.
Receptionist:	Just a moment, please ... Miss Gomez? Look, I can't get anyone to answer on that floor. I'm going to ask someone from the Post Room to escort you up there.
Mr Bristow:	Excuse me Cynthia, but someone has parked in my parking space. Could you do something about it? It's a red Renault and the number is K925 SLC.
Receptionist:	Er, yes Mr Bristow ... er would you like to leave the number with me? I'm a bit tied up. I'll see to it as soon as I have a moment.
Mr Bristow:	Well, I can't leave the car where it is and I can't afford to wait. I have an urgent meeting with John Peters.
Miss Gomez:	Oh, you do, do you? What time was your appointment, if you don't mind me asking.

Mr Bristow:	I beg your pardon? ... 11.15, why?
Miss Gomez:	It doesn't matter. I was just curious. Well, good luck to you. And by the way, that red Renault is mine and I won't be needing your space any more. You're welcome to it and to Mr Peters!
Mr Bristow:	Excuse me ... Just a minute madam! I'm sorry, I didn't realize ...
Delivery man:	Mind your backs please everyone! Excuse me, love, where do these filing cabinets belong then? I was told to bring them to Reception ... They're for ...
Receptionist:	Are they for Mr Peters, by any chance?
Delivery man:	As a matter of fact, they are! So you *were* expecting them then ...
Courier:	Er ... I don't want to be a nuisance, but about this parcel ... *(phone)*
Receptionist:	Good morning. GKK Ltd.
Caller:	I wish to speak to Alison Cooper, and if I have to call again, or if I am cut off again ... *(Bell rings)* Hello? ... Hello? What on earth is going on?
Receptionist:	Er ... excuse me everybody ... It's the fire alarm, would you mind all leaving the building please ... And once we are safely outside, I'll introduce you to John Peters ...

Exercise 8

a I hope you don't mind, but I really can't hang on any longer.
b Hello? What's going on? This music is driving me mad.
c Listen. I would like to make a complaint.
d Excuse me, it's already twenty past four and my appointment was for 4 o'clock.
e There is some equipment missing from my room.
f How much longer do I have to stand here before I get attended to?
g Why doesn't anyone answer the phones in this place?

Exercise 9

a I have come about a complaint received from a member of the public about the conduct of a member of staff on your premises. He is alleged to have displayed insulting behaviour.
b Hello? Listen, I am fed up with being sent the wrong consignments. The invoices are incorrect and the goods don't match.
c Can you put me through to someone I can complain to about a faulty product I've just received. The thing fell apart as soon as I got it out of the box!
d Sorry to bother you, but I must have a word with someone about the way people are driving out of the car park in the evenings.
e The switchboard take absolutely ages to answer in the mornings. Something has to be done about it.

UNIT 11

Speaker 1: Good morning. I hope you will be able to deal with me efficiently and quickly. I am a very busy man, you see, and will need to be on my way by 4.35.

Speaker 2: Hi there. I just love that picture! It's really gorgeous. Listen, could you help me, please? I would like to have a word with Robert de Witte – that's D-E, with a small d, W-I-T-T-E. At least, I guess that's how he spells it. My name is Dolores F. Laine and I am a Managing Consultant.

Speaker 3: Hello ... I'm sorry to bother you ... I was wondering if ... well ... if it would be all right if I waited here while my wife attends a meeting. If it's inconvenient, I don't mind waiting somewhere else. Er, I am not sure how long she will be, or who she is seeing, but I shall be quite happy if I've just got somewhere to sit, out of the way, so to speak ...

Speaker 4: Mr Quirk. I want to see Mr Quirk. I have an appointment fixed for 9.15. The name's Gina Fresco.

Speaker 5: Hi. My name's Franco James. I have a lunch engagement with Lisa Bailey. She's expecting me around now. Could you give her a call for me? Cheers.

USEFUL PHRASES

On the phone

I have (Ms Gomez) in reception for you.
Would you like me to send (her) up?
Can you send someone (down) for (her)?
(He) has an appointment with ...
I'll put you through to ...
Where are you calling from?
Can I put you through to someone else?
The line's busy.
Would you like (him) to call you back?
Can I get (her) to call you back?
I think you have the wrong number.
I'll try another extension for you.
May I ask who's calling?
It will take you about (10 minutes) by taxi.
Go ahead.
You're through.
What's it to do/in connection with? (= What is the nature of your request?)
I am sorry you were cut off.
Would you like to hold?
Hold the line, please.
Could I have your name, please?
Can you spell that?
Can you call back later?
I'll see if (he's) around.
I'll try (extension 445) for you.

Welcoming visitors in person

Would you sign in the book please?
Can I help you?
How can I help you?
I'm afraid (they) can't see you without an appointment.
Would you like to take a seat?
(They) won't be long.
I won't keep you a moment.
(She'll) be down shortly.
Thank you for waiting.
Would you mind waiting a few moments?
(Are they) expecting you?
I'll tell (him) you are here.
Which company do you represent?
I'm afraid (she) is not available.
I'm afraid we don't have anyone by that name here.
I'll be with you as soon as I can.
Could I have your name, please?
Can I get you some refreshment/a drink?
I'll tell (them) you are here.

Explaining unavailability

I'm afraid (she's) off sick today.
I'm sorry, but (he) isn't in today.
Sorry, but (she's) tied up all day.
I'm afraid (he's) in a meeting.

Polite small talk

Isn't the weather awful/wonderful?
Have you come far?
Is it cold outside?
What's it like living in ...?
Whereabouts are you from?

Social responses

That's all right. (reassuring)
Don't worry about it. (reassuring)
Of course (responding positively to an open request, e.g. *May I ... ?*)
Of course not (responding positively to a request, e.g. *Do you mind if ... ?*)
I'll see what I can do. (= I will do my best to help.)
Just a minute.

Miscellaneous

The thing is ... (a common way of beginning to explain something)
As far as I know ... (= I am not totally certain)
I'll enquire whether it has been reported.
I'll arrange for it to be collected.
What seems to be the problem?
I'm sorry. I didn't quite catch that. Could you repeat it please?
Would you like to come this way? (= follow me)
Can you find your way (out)?
I'll tell you what I'll do ...
If all fails ... (= if none of these solutions works ...)
Sorry to bother you, but ...
With it being (the summer holidays) ... (beginning of an excuse)

Making appointments

(He's) fully-booked then.
Would (3 o'clock) suit you?
(He) could probably fit you in.

Apologising

I am sorry.
I *do* apologise.
I'm awfully sorry.
Sorry about that.

ANSWER KEY

NB: The answers to open-ended or inference questions are not provided.

UNIT 1

General responsibilities

1 affect: influence
  secretarial: clerical
  opinion: impression
  do: undertake

2 a entertain guests
  b an interface between the organisation and the outside world
  c operate as relief telephonists
  d enjoy good public relations
  e appointments

3 Because companies need good public relations and their receptionists often give visitors a first impression.

4 In some companies, receptionists operate the switchboard as well as welcome visitors. In others, they don't.

Specific responsibilities

Reading
    1 f 2 g 3 h 4 a 5 b 6 c 7 i 8 k
    9 j 10 d 11 e 12 n 13 m 14 l 15 o

1 office desk area: work station
  building: premises
  accompanying: escorting
  clothing: garments
  illnesses: ailments

Receiving visitors

2 a vacancies
  b regular
  c goods
  d delivery
  e firms

UNIT 2

What makes a good receptionist?

1 a first feelings or opinions
  b skilful use of cosmetics
  c well-spoken: speaking in a refined manner
  d behaviour
  e diplomacy
  f keen
  g tactful

3 *Suggested answers*
  positive image: being helpful and efficient
  first-aid knowledge: ability to help people who are unwell
  good general education: satisfactory standard or results at least up to secondary education
  human relations ability: experience or skills in dealing with people
  ability to engage in easy but discreet conversation: skilled in speaking socially with people

Reception skills

Suggested answers
1 a 2   e 7
  b 3   f 1
  c 5   g 6
  d 4   h 8

The Visitor's Register and the Appointments Book

3 *Suggested answers*
  Sue Lowe is seeing Alexis Thorne at 9 o'clock.
  Sally Wells has an appointment with Jane Fox at 9 o'clock and will need a car pass.
  The KJC representative will see Jon Burch at 9.15, but as Jon is away, M. Bourne will replace him.
  LEX are coming to collect JR's car for a service at 10 o'clock. The keys will be left at the reception desk.

UNIT 3

Knowing your business

Suggested answers

a Sales
b Sales – overseas
c Accounts – sales ledger
d Personnel – recruitment/training
e Corporate
f Operations – mail
g Sales – overseas or Corporate – business management
h Personnel – recruitment and training
i Marketing – research
j Accounts – bought ledger

The receptionist's equipment

a For all visitors to sign in.
b To know who is expected.
c To have all employees' names, departments and nos.
d To understand the company structure.
e For everyday stock and maintenance needs.
f For quick reference in emergencies.
g To find details of local services.
h To keep waiting visitors occupied.
i For enquiries about the company.
j For giving and taking messages.

The internal directory

1 *Suggested answers*

Extract A

Names should be in alphabetical order.
First names should appear for gender identification.
First names should follow the surnames.
Extensions should appear on the right of the names.
Extension 3217 appears twice, although sometimes staff share the same extension number.
Departments and positions could be mentioned after the names.

Extract B

Out of date.
First names should appear for gender identification.
No indication of what the names in bold signify.
Mason and Murray are in the wrong order.
Departments and positions could be mentioned after the names.

3 *Suggested answers*

a	1488 or 3446	f	2987
b	2529	g	1488
c	2578	h	3211
d	1543	i	3689
e	1431 or 1432		

UNIT 4

1 a *Suggested answers*

Positive

Meeting a lot of people
Getting familiar with the company structure/good way to start in business
Keeping secrets

Negative

Hectic
People not knowing who or what they want

b Not telling other people what she/he has been told in confidence.

c variety: a whole range
  correspondence: letters
  busy: hectic
  calm: cool
  a lot of: loads of
  connect: put through to

2 *Suggested answers*

	Duties	Likes	Dislikes
Speaker 1	Answering the phone Telling staff when their visitors arrive and checking bags for security	Dealing with visitors	The monotony of answering the phone Being on his own
Speaker 2	Taking incoming calls and dealing with visitors	Face to face contact Talking to/helping visitors	Not having enough time to talk to visitors
Speaker 3	Switchboard	X	Staff who do not answer their phones

UNIT 5

1

		Appointment with	Time	Special Circumstances
a	Mr Tanaka	Ms Lawson	2.30	He is early for his appointment. He wants the men's room.
b	Ms O'Connor	Brigitte Meyer	10.30	She is a bit late.
c	Mr Deleuse	Jim Hanks for the Committee meeting	11.15	He is not sure who has organised the meeting

2 Could you remind me where the men's room is?
It's nice to see you again.

3 **a** It's nice to see you again.
   b I'll let Ms Lawson know you are here.
   c Can I help you?
   d Could I have your name, please?
   e Would you like to take a seat?

4 **a** I am a *little* early.
   b I am a *bit* late.
   c I *have come for* an 11.15 committee meeting.

5 *Situation A*
   a Ms Jordan would like to see the Personnel Manager.
   b She is not in.
   c By asking the Personnel Manager's assistant to see her.

   d I need some help: *I wonder if you could help me?*
   Mrs Malin is not available: *She's not in this afternoon.*
   I will telephone her assistant: *I'll give her assistant a call.*
   Sit down: *Have a seat.*

Situation B
   a May I ask if *he is expecting* you?
   So I can *let* Mr Hawkins *know* your are here.
   I'll give his secretary *a call* to make sure he's *around.*
   Would you *mind signing* the book?
   He's *got* someone with him?
   c Who do you work for: Which company are you from?
   wait: hold on a moment
   available: around
   coming: on her way down
   OK?: All right?

6

	With app.	Without app.	Postal delivery	Gen. Enquiry	Service Personnel	Temp staff	Job Applicant	Personal	Requirements
a			✓						Sign for receipt
b								✓	Inform Mary Salina that her friend has arrived
c								✓	Aspirins needed
d								✓	Shopping
e					✓				Window cleaning
f							✓		Temp for Mrs Angelica
g					✓				Park van for unloading
h	✓								Kept waiting
i		✓							Freelance designer to see someone in marketing
j							✓		Seeing Mr Schrand

8 **a** false **d** false
   b false **e** false
   c true   **f** true

9 **a** Sign the register.
   b Certainly.
   c And there's one other thing.
   d He's not in today.
   e The line's engaged.
   f Will you hold?
   g Who's calling?
   h What was it you wanted?
   i I won't keep you a moment.
   j Don't ask me.

UNIT 6

1 **a** He cannot keep his appointment with Ruth Atkins and he'd like her to phone back to arrange another meeting.
   b She wants to know whether there is a branch in Brussels.
   c Debbie Dickinson has not replied to any of his faxes and as he is going to be away, there will be no one around to take any calls.
   d She is probably doing some design work for an advertisement.
   e 0171-794 5643. She should ring this number if there is a problem about collecting her Swiss Air ticket.
   f Sandy is probably an employee in the company and works with Penny.

2 *Suggested answers*
   a Patrick Ermoy called for Ruth Atkins (Production). He can't make tomorrow's meeting. Pls call.
   b Francis Rodgers (3468754) wants to know if we have office in Brussels. Pls call.
   c Peter Sutton (Area Manager E. Europe) called Debbie Dickinson. Needs reply by Friday 20th re her visit. Urgent, as he won't be available after tomorrow.
   d Liz Saunders (Dolphin Design) called Shireen or Joe (advertising). Pls call tomorrow before 10.

e Premier Travel (Robert Day) called Betty Goldberg: air ticket to Geneva will be ready at Swiss Air desk 8 am onwards tomorrow. Call 0171 794 5643 if problem.

f Sandy from Credit Control called Penny. Won't be in tomorrow. Sick. Expecting to return Monday.

Action

a Give message to Ruth Atkins.

b Ask or pass message to Sales Dept if not sure of answer.

c Ensure Debbie Dickinson gets message today or tomorrow.

d Give message to Shireen or Joe.

e Ensure Betty Goldberg gets message today.

f Give message to Penny in Credit Control. Inform Personnel (?)

4 a I won't be in.

b Perhaps she could call me to reschedule.

c I won't be able to make tomorrow's meeting.

d Something has come up.

e There won't be anyone around.

f Could someone call me back?

5 *Suggested answers*

a He spelt the caller's name incorrectly and he wrote down the wrong date and time.

b He did not mention where Gavin Costner's wife is spending the next few days, or that he should buy Eau de Toilette and not perfume. Perfume also spelt wrongly.

c He did not take the name of the caller or request details of the faulty equipment.

d He forgot to mention there will not be any video facilities in the room.

6 a off-sick

b I'll take care of it for you/I'll make sure ...

c If all fails

d get hold of

e go ahead

f would do

7 a Of course.

b Of course not.

c I'm afraid not. Sorry. Not over the phone.

d I'll put you through to her assistant.

e May I ask who's calling?

f Yes. Where are you coming from?

g About 10 minutes by taxi.

h That's all right

i I think you have the wrong number.

j I'm sorry. I'll try another extension.

UNIT 7

1 *Suggested answers:* See table below.

	Name of caller	Person/dept requested	Nature of request
a	Helmut Wertz	Sales/Customer Service	Availability of models
b	Sophie Boyard	Geoffrey Palmer	Tell Palmer she's late for appointment
c	X	Ms Jackson	Directions to drive to offices
d	X	Georgina	Wrong number?
e	X	X	Possibility for a work training attachment
f	X	Brian Bradfield	Not getting through to the department
g	Christos Pantos free lance artist	Head of Design	He'd like to see Judy Thompson
h	Fiona Earle	Carla	Appointment with Carla for a haircut and highlights
i	X	Dr Talbot	Appointment as soon as possible
j	Mrs Hanson	Husband	She would like to speak to him.

3 I'll put you through to ...

The receptionist will connect the caller to the person required.

Is it to do with ...?

The receptionist enquires about the subject of the request.

He's fully booked.

The receptionist confirms that the person is not free.

Would 3 o'clock suit you?

The receptionist checks that the time is acceptable.

Just call in any time.

You can visit us when you like.

As far as I know.

The receptionist is not 100% sure.

We don't have anyone by that name.

The receptionist confirms that the person doesn't work in the building.

I'll see what I can do.

The receptionist will do his/her best.

4 a I have a question about the *availability of one of* your models.

b Could you possibly *let them know?*

c You might *just have to keep* trying.

d Thank *you for calling* Scorpio.

e Any *particular time?*

f He could probably *fit you in* if you could *get here straight away.*

5 *Suggested answers*

The receptionist thinks the caller is asking when Chris Chang will get back from Korea. In fact, the caller wants the receptionist to give him a message on his return.

Other mistakes:

Mr Chang is not in office today.
He get back tomorrow.

6 a No. She runs our Belgian operation.

b Don't worry. I'll sort it out.

c I'll see that it's forwarded.

d They are seven hours ahead.

e I'm sorry I cut you off. I'll put you through again.

f I'll enquire whether it has been reported.

g He reports to Mrs Saunders.

h I'll arrange for it to be collected.

i Would you like me to get her to call you back?

j I'll see if it's been handed in.

k What is it in connection with?

l I'm sorry. I didn't quite catch that.

UNIT 8

1 a John Peters

b John Peters' extension does not answer and he has not come down to meet Miss Gomez.

c She wants to speak to John Peters.

2 a Sorry to bother you again.

b Are you understaffed or something?

c I'm sorry you're being kept waiting.

d Look here!

e I'm awfully sorry. The thing is, the lines are very busy at the moment.

4 a i   **b** ii   **c** ii   **d** ii

5 *Suggested answers*

a A signature for Mr Peters' parcel.

b By asking someone from the Post Room to escort her to John Peters' office.

c Someone had parked in his parking space.

d To leave.

e (Answers will vary.)

f The fire alarm provides the receptionist with a very good excuse for ending the phone calls. It will also make John Peters come down and meet his visitors.

6 a I'm a bit tied up.

b All I can suggest is ...

c I do apologise.

d I've got someone on the line for Alison.

e Well, can you take the call please?

7 **a** I don't want to be a *nuisance* but about this parcel ...
b Are they for Mrs Peters, by any *chance*?
c Isn't there anyone *else* free?
d I will personally *ensure* she gets the message.
e I can't *afford* to wait.
f And by the *way*, that red Renault is mine.
g As a matter of *fact*, they are!

8 **a** Of course not. I fully understand.
b I'm afraid it's still engaged. Can you still hold, or would you like to call back later?
c What seems to be the problem?
d I'm sorry. I'll remind them again for you.
e I'm terribly sorry to hear that. I'll notify the security guard.
f I'll be with you just as soon as I can.
g With it being the holiday period, we are a bit understaffed.

9 *Suggested answers:* See table below

UNIT 9

1

Name of visitor: *Juan Santos*

Position and Company: *Sales Director, Candea, Barcelona*

Appointment with: *Ms Mason*

Time of appointment: *9 o'clock*

Notes: *Visitor a bit late. Left suitcase at reception. Needs taxi after meeting.*

	Complaint	Report/direct to	
a	Insulting behaviour of member of staff	Sales Manager Customer Service Manager Production Manager	Personnel Manager ✔ Security Operations
b	Customer getting incorrect goods	Sales Manager Customer Service Manager ✔ Production Manager	Personnel Manager Security Operations
c	Customer got faulty product	Sales Manager Customer Service Manager Production Manager ✔	Personnel Manager Security Operations
d	Staff's standard of driving when leaving car park	Sales Manager Customer Service Manager Production Manager	Personnel Manager Security ✔ Operations
e	Long time for switchboard to answer calls	Sales Manager Customer Service Manager Production Manager	Personnel Manager Security Operations ✔

a *Who are you?*
　Could I have your name please?
Where do you work?
　Which company are you from?
What time?
　May I ask the time of (your appointment)?
Sit down.
　Take a seat
Someone will see you soon.
　(Her assistant) will be down shortly.
Why are you here?
　Would you mind explaining what it was that you were seeing her about?

b i　May I ask if you have an appointment?
　ii　Could you give me your name?
　iii　Which company do you represent?
　iv　Would you mind signing in the Visitor's Register?
　v　Sorry. I didn't (quite) catch that. Could you repeat it please?

2　*Suggested answers*
Can I go up to Corporate?
　Are they expecting you?
I'm sorry I'm late.
　That's all right.
I'm here for a meeting with John Hanks.
　What time was it for?
I've come to see the Production Controller.
　Do you have an appointment?
My name's Tanaka.
　How can we help you?
I wonder if you could help me?
　Certainly.
I want to see the people in Accounts.
　May I ask what it's about?

4　*Suggested answers*
Apologising
I am sorry. I don't know.
Sorry to keep you waiting.
I am afraid she can't see you without an appointment.

Giving instructions
The ladies' room is over there, on the left.

Offering help or service
Can I order you a taxi?
I'll let him know you are here.
Would you like to come this way?
Can I take your coat?
Can I get you anything?
I'll have a look for you.
Would you mind waiting a moment?

Greeting
It's nice to see you again.
Hello. Can I help you?
Please take a seat.

Making enquiries
Do you have an appointment?
Can I have your name please?
Can you find your way?

Giving information
She won't be a minute.

5　1 d　2 a　3 b　4 c

6　*Suggested answers*
a　Can I help you?
　Can I have your name please?
　Who is your appointment with?
　Thank you. I'll just let her/him know you are here.
　Hello. I have Mr Hanbury in reception for you. Can you come to collect him?/Can he come (up)?
　OK. It's room 657.
b　Hello. Can I help you?
　That's all right. Would you sign in the Visitor's Book, please?
　Don't worry about that/You can leave that/No problem. Can I get you anything?
　Miss Relton will be down to see you shortly.
　She's Frank Timms' assistant.
c　I am sorry about this.
　You wanted to see Mike Weeks didn't you?/Your appointment was with Mike Weeks, wasn't it?
　Right. It's Mr (Bakasi) isn't it? From RJS Software?
　OK. Sorry. I'll remind them for you.

d Do you have an appointment?
Well, I don't think they'll be able to see you without an appointment. Even so, they're very busy. What company are you from?
I am sorry. I don't think we can help you. Why don't you make an appointment?
No, I don't think that would be a good idea. I tell you what, I'll give the Personnel Department a call and see if they can help.

7 *Suggested answers*
a How can we help you?
b You needn't worry about that.
c Can I get you anything while you are waiting?
d Sorry to keep you waiting.
e Would you mind filling in the details in the book?
f May I ask you not to park there and to move your car to the multi-storey car park?
g They won't be a minute.
h Do you know how to get to Mr Zena's office?
i Would you like to leave your luggage at reception?
j I'm afraid the Manager is not available without an appointment.

8 *Suggested answers*
Where are you from?
From the north, originally.
Your English is very good.
Thank you.
I would love to be able to speak a foreign language like that.
If you live in the country, you pick it up quickly.
Isn't it a horrible day today?
Yes. Awful.
Is it cold outside?
It's not too bad. A bit chilly.
Where do you live exactly?
Right in the centre of town.
How long have you been with the company?

For about five years
Do you like working here?
Yes, I do.
How are you doing?
I'm fine. And you?
What's it like over there?
It's not bad.

9 *Suggested answers*
a Would you mind filling in the Visitor's Register?
taking a seat?
leaving the bags at reception?
making an appointment?
speaking more slowly?
waiting there?
not smoking in the reception area?
coming back later?
telling me what it is about?
not pushing in?
b Could you tell me who you are?
what time your appointment is?
what your business is?/what you want?
where you are going?
what company you are from?
if they are expecting you?
what you are responsible for?
who you wish to speak to?

10 *Suggested answers*
a Jeanette Bolton is supposed to be out of her meeting by 12 noon. Would you mind waiting, Mr Gualco? She suggests you have your discussions over lunch.
b Personnel are behind schedule with their interviews. I am sorry Mrs von Heijne, but your session is rescheduled for 11.20. Is that all right?
c The strategy meeting is now in Jeremy's room, at the same time. You can go on up, Mr Knuchel, if you like. Coffee is being served.
d Work stations 2001 to 2050 in the West Wing are now ready for installation. You can get the keys from Dorothy.

UNIT 10

2 *Suggested answers*
Plan 1

a Go through the double doors and they are first on your right.
b Yes. Through the double doors, past the toilets. You'll find them in the rest room.
c Through the double doors and you'll see them opposite you, next to the toilets.
d Yes, there is. At the far end of the canteen.
e Through there, in the Post Room, by the stairs.
f Through the double doors and you'll see the toilets on the left.

Plan 2

a Yes. To your left, turn right along the corridor and there's a snack bar opposite the shop.
b To the left, down the corridor, first right into Secretariat and you'll find the conference room on the left.
c Down the corridor and it's first right and first left. Opposite the toilets.
d Yes. Go right along that corridor and you'll find Room 5 near the end, on your left.
e Carry on to the end of the corridor on your left, turn right at the end, and the library entrance is on your right, just past the conference room.
f Go along this corridor to my right and you'll find the lifts facing you at the end, between the stairs and the fire exit.

3 *Suggested answers*
a Follow me, please.
b There's one on the corner.
c Would you like me to order you one?
d She won't be long now.
e It's yesterday's. OK?
f No. This is number 342. Try further down.

g Sorry. We couldn't get hold of you to let you know.
h I can't recommend it personally, but a lot of our overseas staff stay there.
i Whereabouts are you going?
j You needn't be nervous. They're ever so nice.
k You'd better see someone in Operations.
l Who is it for?
m Nothing's been reported. I'll keep a look out.
n I'm afraid you can't leave it there.
o Those are not for sale, I'm afraid.
p Your best bet would be the chain store opposite.
q I haven't got any change. Sorry.

4 *Suggested answers*
a It looks like there is something missing.
b I'm afraid you can't go up unless you have an appointment.
c We need your number in case we have to call you back about any time changes.
d Provided you haven't parked in a reserved space, it should be OK.
e Someone may have handed it in to the security guard.
f I will have someone send it up.
g When you get out of the lift, you will see it facing you.
h They are located round the back of the photocopier at the end of the corridor.
i There aren't any shops around here.

5 a Oaktree and Co
b Loddon and Loddon Ltd
c 5th October 1995
d Speedway International Express
e Artwork
f One
g Courier

6 Hello. This *is the reception* desk. A package *has arrived for* you via *Speedway* from *Loddon and Loddon Ltd*. I *have signed* for it and *I've* examined it. I think it is the *package* you've been waiting for.

UNIT 11

2

Physique	Hair	Clothes	Speech
tall	short	suit	talkative
short	curly	overcoat	quietly-spoken
heavily-built	straight	loose-fitting	blunt
thin	bald(ing)	jeans	sexy
young	long	jacket	loud
good-looking	wavy	tight-fitting	concise
old	fair(haired)	shirt	accent
middle-aged	pony tail	hat	
attractive	grey	scruffy	
elderly	(dark) haired	elegant	
limp		blouse	
		tee shirt	
		skirt	
		smart	

Attitude/Personality	Facial characteristics	Belongings
friendly	(brown)eyes	umbrella
arrogant	thin	briefcase
shy	good-looking	carrier bag
cheerful	plain	box
serious	made-up	
nervous	attractive	
easy-going	tanned	
charming	pale	
cool	moustache	
sexy	beard	
unpleasant	glasses	
vague	square	
sophisticated		
attractive		
blunt		
demanding		
polite		
impolite/rude		
precise		
fair		

3 *Suggested answers*

a A tall, pale man, with grey hair, glasses and an American accent, carrying a briefcase.
b A curly, blonde haired woman in tight-fitting jeans, with a carrier bag.
c An unpleasant, smart young man with curly hair and a beard, wearing a suit.
d A quietly-spoken elderly lady with wavy grey hair.

4 *Suggested answers*
Picture 1 He's a middle-aged man with brown hair, glasses and a moustache
Picture 2 She's an attractive, smartly dressed young woman, with blonde hair.
Picture 3 He's a pleasant, smart young man with curly brown hair, wearing a suit.
Picture 4 She's a cheerful and friendly woman, smartly dressed with dark hair.
Picture 5 He's a pleasant, smartly dressed man with a beard, wearing glasses.
Picture 6 She's a quietly spoken, middle-aged woman, with fair hair.

5 *Suggested answers*

Speaker 1	Speaker 2	Speaker 3	Speaker 4	Speaker 5
arrogant	talkative	hesitant	concise	cool
German?	American	shy	Italian?	sexy
precise	loud	vague		

6 a 2 **b** 5 **c** 4 **d** 1 **e** 3

UNIT 12

2 *Suggested answers*
   a See example.
   b Is that Mary Wilson? This is the reception desk. Jane, from Apex recruitment, called at 11 o'clock and would like you to call her. She wants to know if you have any vacancies that need filling.
   c Someone from Skandecor called at 4.20 to see if we were interested in purchasing some office furniture. They'll call again.
   d Joan? I've got a message for you from Jackie, in Personnel. There's a snag with next week's management course. Someone has dropped out. She wants to know if you can suggest a replacement. It's rather urgent.
   e Is that Mike Cragg? Penny Tranter called just after 2.30, to enquire about the latest news on the production schedule. She also wanted to know if the June 17 visit is still on. She asked if you would call her.
   f Pauline? A Hans Meyer called you at ten to twelve, but didn't leave a message or number I am afraid.

4 *Suggested answers*
   a Felicity Worsley called to say she will/would be late today.
   b Greg Johns asked you to call him as soon as possible.
   c Kate Fleming phoned to say she had seen the overseas reps after all.
   d Emiko wants to know if you can keep the first week in August free.
   e Jan Laarsson said he will/would be arriving on Wednesday 5 at about 2 o'clock.
   f Tulin Aksu wants to know when the sales meeting is rescheduled for.
   g Eric Hutson promised he will/would send the report in two days.
   h Tina Poulos wondered if someone could send her an updated price list.
   i Nancy Baker called to say she didn't manage/hadn't managed to see Harumi.
   j Hank O'Keefe wanted to make sure you don't/didn't forget to bring some disks.

5 *Suggested answers*
   a She asked what time the Accounts Department closed.
   b He asked you to call him back after 4 o'clock.
   c She complained that you haven't/hadn't even replied to her last two letters.
   d He wondered why you didn't/don't spend more on promotion.
   e She suggested you dropped/drop Marcus Grainger a line.
   f He said he will/would leave after lunch.
   g She asked if Charles was in today.
   h He wondered how sales were doing.
   i She told you not to worry about the presentation/She said you shouldn't worry about the presentation, and said she would have it ready by tonight if you'd like to call her.
   j She requested the overseas address of Jana Masson.

6 *Suggested answers*
  a He told you not to be late.
  b He suggested you should ignore it.
  c He asked you to call him back.
  d They said they wouldn't be long.
  e She said she would reply by fax.
  f He wondered whether the modems were compatible.

7 **a** 5 **b** 4 **c** 9 **d** 7 **e** 8 **f** 3 **g** 10
  h 1 **i** 2 **j** 6

8 **a** What kind of information?
  b Can you give me some more details?
  c We have several people by that name. Do you have her other name?
  d Who's calling, please? I'll ask his secretary.
  e Your first-aid officer on that floor is Mary Fletcher, but I can call a doctor if you like.

9 **a** Hang on/Please wait a moment/Hold the line please/Putting you through/The line's engaged/Will you hold?/Can you spell that?/Are you trying to sell us something?/I can't understand a word you are saying/Can you call back later?/I'll make a note of it/I have a Ms Rodrigues on the line/Sorry to keep you waiting/Just a minute/Who's calling?/May I have your number?/What is it about?/I'll try another extension/What?/What company are you from?/I'll enquire whether anyone has seen it/them

  c *Suggested answers*
  Hang on.
    Hold the line please.
  Okey dokey.
    All right/fine/OK.
  See you.
    Goodbye.
  Sorry, dunno.
    I am sorry, I don't know.
  I can't understand a word you are saying.
    I am sorry. I don't understand.
  Ta ta.
    Goodbye.
  What?
    I beg your pardon/Sorry?